Greetings!

Enjoy this first issue of **Vintage Notions Monthly**. It continues to share the work of Mary Brooks Picken and the Woman's Institute which inspired my book *Vintage Notions: An Inspirational Guide to Needlework, Cooking, Sewing, Fashion and Fun!*

All my life I have been fascinated by fashion, sewing and all things vintage. As the owner of Indygo Junction, a sewing pattern company, and author of a library of craft books, I have spent a lot of time researching sewing publications that have been released throughout the years. It was during this research that I came upon a name that would have a huge impact on my career, Mary Brooks Picken.

A pioneer in the sewing arts, Mary Brooks Picken was the author of almost 100 needlework, sewing, and textile books. Regarded as an authority on dress, design, and sewing, she founded the Woman's Institute of Domestic Arts and Sciences (1916-1932) in Scranton, PA. At one point the institute had an enrollment of 300,000 women across the world connected through its correspondence courses and publications.

Why create a Vintage Notions Monthly?

When I read the story of Mary Brooks Picken and started to grasp the magnitude of her influence, I was compelled to collect and archive her numerous works. I believe I now have acquired the largest collection of Woman's Institute publications in the world. Although this Institute was founded 100 years ago, the treasure trove of lessons and stories are still relevant today and offer a blueprint for living a contented life. To celebrate the 100th anniversary of this influential institute, what better way than to introduce the material to a modern community than with the internet? (I think Mary would be thrilled!)

Inside the pages of this magazine you will find articles on sewing, cooking, decorating and even upcycling as well as testimonials from students. An original issue of the *Inspiration* newsletter is combined with articles I curate from *Fashion Service*, another popular Woman's Institute publication. I also add a "Magic Pattern" each month for those of you who are looking for quick and easy sewing projects! In this inaugural issue several pages of promotional content are included to give you a window back in time to a student's perspective.

I invite you to join our online community. Visit my blog at amybarickman.com,
join my Facebook page & Instagram- amybarickmanstudio,
and my Facebook group- amybarickmansvintagemademodern.

So Enjoy! Be Inspired! Get creative!

All my best, *Amy*

$\mathcal{T}$he image you see above was the original cover for this issue of Inspiration from January 1920. I chose to update *Vintage Notions Monthly* for a more modern look using a cover from the January 1928 issue of Fashion Service. The graphic, art deco style which was so popular during this time still makes a statement today!

The Woman's Institute
WHAT IT IS

THE Woman's Institute of Domestic Arts and Sciences of Scranton, Pennsylvania, is an educational institution for women. It was founded for the purpose of making a practical knowledge of the domestic arts and sciences available to every woman or girl, wherever she may live.

Many of our schools and colleges are now teaching such subjects as dressmaking, millinery, and cooking. But the vast majority of women do not realize the need or value of a knowledge of such subjects until they are beyond school ages or have taken up the duty of presiding over a home, and even then comparatively few can spare the time and money necessary to attend a resident school.

It was this condition which led the Woman's Institute to develop an entirely new method of teaching these subjects by which any woman or girl, no matter where she may live or how she may be situated, may learn at her own convenience right in her own home.

The Woman's Institute is associated with the International Correspondence Schools of Scranton, Pennsylvania, and its method of teaching is based on the I.C.S. home-study method by which technical and commercial subjects have been successfully taught for more than a quarter of a century.

More than twenty thousand members have learned or are now learning through the Institute to make their own clothes or have prepared to take up dressmaking or millinery as a business. Hundreds more are joining the Institute every month. The present membership includes more than eight thousand home women, fourteen hundred dressmakers, six hundred teachers, and thousands of business women, girls at school or college, girls employed in offices, stores and factories, and women and girls in many other occupations. They live in every state in the Union. Many are in foreign countries. And all are learning right at home and receiving by mail the same intimate help and attention from expert teachers that they would receive if they were assembled in one great classroom.

The Woman's Institute brings a new opportunity of great possibilities to the women of America.

Its coming means the way to a skilled trade or profession—with easier, pleasanter work at better pay—for thousands upon thousands of women and girls who earn their own living.

It means better and neater garments for mother, wife, and daughter at less cost for clothes.

It means more efficient housewives, more attractive homes, and happier families.

It means a new dawn in the homes of the nation—a new day in the lives of its womanhood.

Originally published in "Dressmaking, Millinery and Cooking Made Easy" , 1916

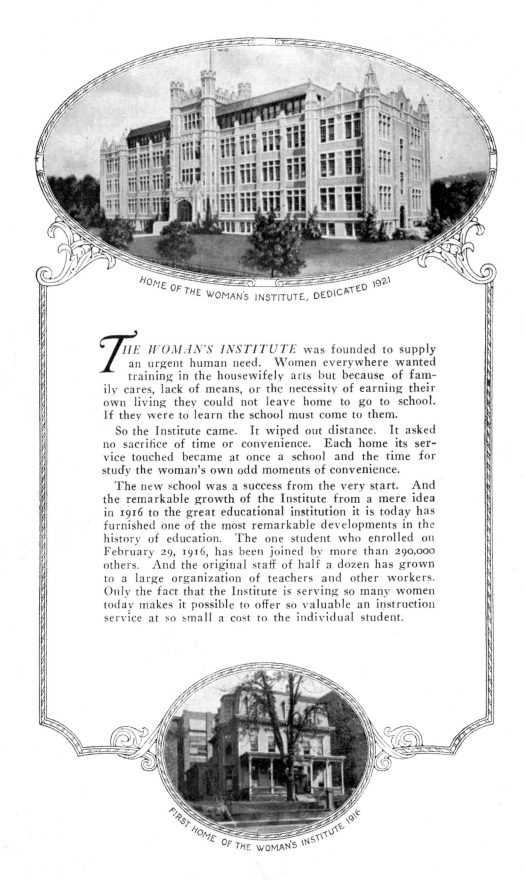

HOME OF THE WOMAN'S INSTITUTE, DEDICATED 1921

THE WOMAN'S INSTITUTE was founded to supply an urgent human need. Women everywhere wanted training in the housewifely arts but because of family cares, lack of means, or the necessity of earning their own living they could not leave home to go to school. If they were to learn the school must come to them.

So the Institute came. It wiped out distance. It asked no sacrifice of time or convenience. Each home its service touched became at once a school and the time for study the woman's own odd moments of convenience.

The new school was a success from the very start. And the remarkable growth of the Institute from a mere idea in 1916 to the great educational institution it is today has furnished one of the most remarkable developments in the history of education. The one student who enrolled on February 29, 1916, has been joined by more than 290,000 others. And the original staff of half a dozen has grown to a large organization of teachers and other workers. Only the fact that the Institute is serving so many women today makes it possible to offer so valuable an instruction service at so small a cost to the individual student.

FIRST HOME OF THE WOMAN'S INSTITUTE 1916

Originally published in "Cookery Made Easy" pamphlet , 1932

A Monthly Visitor
You Will Always Enjoy

Many of our readers tell us that the Woman's Institute Magazine is a genuine inspiration to them. And what its intimate, helpful monthly visits will mean to you can be better expressed in the words of our readers themselves. So you will find here just a few of the many thousands of enthusiastic comments received at the Woman's Institute:

Thank you for sending my copy of *Inspiration*, as it certainly is a very bright spot in my life and I would not be without it. I am enclosing money for another year's subscription.
MRS. LILLIAN FLYNN,
Cleveland, Ohio.

I take several woman's magazines, but none of them is so helpful as *Inspiration* which always has some article which is just what I am wanting to know about. I had so long wanted to know the right way of a welt pocket and along came *Inspiration* with explicit directions. When I wondered about little Mary's dress along came a page of good ideas. The "how of lamp shades," sofa cushions, "making a dress of a discarded suit," and oh, so many good things it has brought me. I just wouldn't be without it. Every month it comes brimful of information which seems to be exactly what I need.
MRS. LUCY CAMPBELL,
Conklin, N. Y.

One of the prettiest dresses I ever made was from materials and directions described in *Inspiration*. I hope I will never have to be without it.
MRS. HARRIET M. STEWART, De Land, Fla.

Inspiration is fine. I learned how to make good pie crust at last; the first issue I received showed me how.
Mrs. Marian B. Johnson, Lost Creek, Wash.

A New Kind
of Fashion Magazine

Fashion Service, pictured above, is unique among fashion magazines in that it not only brings you the choicest designs of the season, but gives you helpful instructions and suggestions for making them. It will not only serve as a dependable guide, but a helpful dress-making instructor as well.

Readers Endorse Fashion Service

The part that *Fashion Service* plays in making correct and becoming clothes possible for those who receive it is indicated by these enthusiastic endorsements of subscribers:

My copy of *Fashion Service* just received. It seems as though each new copy is a little more wonderful than the last, if that could be possible.
MRS. OLIVE A. DRITCH,
Seattle, Wash.

I find *Fashion Service* very helpful indeed in my work as clothing specialist. I think that it has in it more practical and valuable suggestions for the woman who sews than most fashion magazines.
MARION L. TUCKER,
Massachusetts Agricultural College, Amherst, Mass.

I think *Fashion Service* is the most sensible and practical fashion book I have ever seen. I know that it is going to be a great help to me. MRS. EDYTH JOHNSON,
New York, N. Y.

I would not be without *Fashion Service*, for it contains the cream of the fashions, with the extreme sifted out, or, shall I say, adapted to the needs of the average woman.
MRS. RAY HODGES, Pratt, Kans.

I would hardly know what to do without *Fashion Service* now. It is an indispensable help in planning clothes. My husband thinks I do nothing but study my fashion book, as he calls it, but he is very proud of the garments I make.
MRS. JAMES MOULDS, Detroit, Mich.

Originally published in "Hundreds of Dainty Things for Yourself & Your Home" Sales Insert

MRS. S. JEFFERSON BLAINE
Formerly Miss Dorothy Harmeling
FAIRVIEW, N. J.

And Now, as a Final Word,
We Present the Testimony of

Women Who Know

Students of the Woman's Institute who tell you, from actual experience, what they KNOW these fascinating Courses Can do for YOU.

Back in February 1916, Dorothy Harmeling of Brooklyn, N. Y., was in much the same position that you are now—asking the same questions—wondering whether the Woman's Institute really could teach her to make smart, becoming clothes she would be proud to wear. And on February 29, she enrolled for our course in Dressmaking and Designing and became the first student of the Woman's Institute. And now, after eighteen years, we shall ask Miss Harmeling, now Mrs. S. Jefferson Blaine, of Fairview, N. J., to tell you what she thinks of the Woman's Institute.

What Our First Student Says

I look back on the hours spent with my Woman's Institute course as the most delightful experience of my life. Pretty, becoming clothes for business, for my good times, and for my mother, and now for my own little family, are my reward for the effort put into my course. Two winter coats are my latest achievements, one tan and blue check with a brown fur collar for sports wear, and a lovely blue suede cloth with gray wolf collar and cuffs copied from a Vogue model. This coat cost me exactly $25.00 and I could not have bought it for less than $55.00. I would not be without this training for anything." MRS. DOROTHY HARMELING BLAINE

A Message From the Class of 1920

"In looking through a magazine several days ago, I saw an advertisement of the Woman's Institute. I decided then I just must write you and tell you again how very much the Institute has meant to me. My diploma is dated April 12, 1920, and I am so proud of it. I shall never forget your kind and encouraging letters—I still have every one of them—as well as all the certificates from each lesson.

If every young woman could realize how thorough your courses are and what a wonderful help that knowledge of sewing has been to me through the years, she would take this training if at all possible.

I get so much enjoyment out of sewing—and I didn't care for it especially until I took my course. Without this training I couldn't have one-half the clothes I have now. Last summer, for instance, I made five smart little organdie dresses and the cost of the entire five was less than $6.50. I want to extend to the Woman's Institute my best wishes and grateful appreciation for the help I received."
MISS MARGARET RIDOUT,
Annapolis, Md.

Earns $930 and Does Own Housework

"My course in Dressmaking and Designing has been a joy to study and of untold value to me. I feel so much more capable. I can finish my work more easily, and it has so much more smartness and style than before. And, naturally, my earnings have increased. I have earned $930 in one year besides doing all my own housework. I have splendid success with everything I undertake." MRS. MINNIE BRASHEAR,
North Pleasanton, Texas

Now Has Many More Pretty Clothes

"I am going on a visit to California and have been busy making clothes for myself and my little girl. I have made lingerie, dresses, coats and a lovely suit. I'm so proud of everything and we have two or three times as many pretty things as would otherwise be possible. A beautiful dress coat that would have cost nearly $75 in a Fifth Avenue Shop actually cost less than twenty dollars. And I copied a French evening dress for less than ten dollars that would have cost two or three times as much." MRS. DOROTHY BREARTY,
Brooklyn, N. Y.

Oregon Student Earns Home and Car

"I have found that the Professional Dressmaking Course of the Woman's Institute contains everything needed to carry on a successful business. Best of all, it has given me an opportunity to earn money at home during spare time. It has made possible for me the pleasure of driving my own car and owning the attractive home shown in the accompanying photograph, which, a few years ago, would have seemed beyond my wildest anticipations. The money I put into this Course was certainly the *best investment I ever made*."

MRS. DAVE DIXON,
Portland, Ore.

Page Thirty-Two

Originally published in "Smart Individuality" pamphlet , 1932

Getting a New Start

BY THE EDITOR

Edited by GUSTAVE L. WEINSS

WELL, 1920 is here and on its way. The coming of a new year is to many of us a common enough occurrence. Still those who do not have faith in the hope that the new year has something good in store for us are in the minority. At the beginning of a new year we have a vivid conviction of the duties and obligations in which we have failed, and the moments of self-accusation that come to us as we reflect are valuable. They seem to say to us, "Try again." They make us feel that a new start is precisely what we need to bring to a successful termination many of the things we have set out to accomplish.

AND that is the point on which I wish to dwell —getting a new start. The determination to try again is without doubt the greatest factor for success in the lives of all whose achievements are noteworthy. The courage, the indomitable spirit, to start again after disappointments, losses, failures, and disasters has made possible the success of individuals, the perfection of institutions, the reconstruction of cities, the restoration of nations.

So we can do well to bear these things in mind as we make our pilgrimage through life, for just as an oasis permits the desert traveler to refresh himself on his way, so will a new start enable us to go on our way encouraged, reinvigorated, and determined to dare and do.

SINCE the great war, nation after nation has had to make a new start, and while some are building on a rock others are simply "riding for a fall."

We know that agitation and unrest and greed obstruct the attempts of those who would reconstruct and restore. We know that in the effort to bring order out of disorder there will be victories and defeats and successes and failures. And we know, too, that more new starts will be made and that eventually right will prevail.

Already we can see the beginning of definite steps to maintain law and order, to uphold liberty and justice, and to encourage industry and thrift. And they will continue to wield an influence that will result in the complete restoration of that great remedy for many evils—common-sense.

Then there will be another start and *true* prosperity—that is, prosperity tempered with contentment—will be in the ascendency and ready to reign supreme.

AND as with nations, so with individuals. Since the termination of hostilities thousands of men and women both in and out of the service have had to make a new start.

For some, the lessons taught by war have made clear the career that they wish to establish for themselves, have shown that endeavor is the guiding star of achievement.

In others, these lessons have created indifference, a disinclination to heed the call of the day, namely, productiveness. They have failed to recognize that present-day unrest is due in a large measure to the extraordinary demand for everything that can be produced or for service that can be rendered.

To the former much praise is due. To the latter must and will come an awakening, for they are bound eventually to realize that a secure and prosperous future entails the discarding of the abnormal for the normal and the bringing about of soberness and thrift.

SO, AS the new year advances, let us all try to recognize and utilize the wonderful possibilities of getting a new start.

A new start will help us to bear our trials and tribulations and overcome them. It will soothe and conquer our fears and worries. It will help us deliver ourselves from indifference and inspire us to real endeavor. It will instil in us the courage and determination to win. It will urge us on to the performance of acts and deeds that will be for the betterment of ourselves and thereby for the betterment of those who must associate with us.

Smart Effects *via* Little Things

By MARY BROOKS PICKEN

Director of Instruction and Principal of
School of Dressmaking and Tailoring

IDEALS are necessary regarding life and all it holds—home, church, friends, work, and play. We must have certain ideals about all these vital things and must keep them in the proper place in our minds so that they will make our travels through life pleasant and profitable for us. This business of life starts me thinking many times in my anxiety to render service to all of you, for sometimes I find myself so totally absorbed in the details of the day that I miss seeing the sun and the smiles and hearing the cheery words of encouragement.

ONLY the day before Christmas I was busy trying to get so many letters out to those who seemed to need some word from me that I was entirely tired and, may I admit, a little discouraged. Just at the close of the day my Secretary came in with dozens of beautiful cards and letters— holly, mistletoe, cedar, violets, oranges, and all manner of colors, shapes, and sizes of Christmas cheer. And right then I spent one of the happiest hours of my life, just drinking in the thoughtfulness of you dear, dear folks whom I so eagerly strive to serve. My ideals all took on a new light. My gratitude gave me happiness. I finished the old year and started the new one with bigger hopes and more ambitious plans for all of you than I ever had before.

So in my first 1920 message to you I am going to talk about the little things in dressmaking, because taking care of the little things will make it possible for you to develop garments that are in keeping with your ideals and that will really reward you for the time and energy you expend on them.

THE other day I was talking to a dressmaker who said, "You know, everything I do looks amateurish. I don't understand why, either, for I try very hard to have the dresses I make look right." I realized as I noted her own dress that she was not careful about the little things. And then I wondered about you, my friends. How many of you realize the importance of the little things in dressmaking that make for success, for distinctive garments, garments that you are always proud to wear?

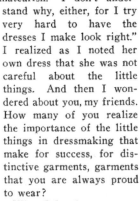

When I first began to sew, I was much concerned when people who knew would look over my work, for I was always sure they could see errors in my workmanship, errors that existed because of my ignorance. The fear of critical eyes made me set

out to learn some definite sewing principles that would carry a garment through to completion without its showing "apprentice stitches."

To build a house, one must have first a plot and a plan, then materials and tools, and then patience. And that reminds me, the other day a student wrote that to make a hat one must have "Pins, Patience, and Picken." So to make a dress, we must have a design; then we must have materials of a color and texture to correspond with the design and to harmonize with the individual and be appropriate for the need; and then we must take heed of the little things that make for success in dressmaking.

IN CUTTING, we should have a pattern that is as nearly correct as possible. We should lay the material out carefully on a smooth surface and then observe the following rules:

Place each pattern piece on a correct grain of the material. In almost all standard garments, the lengthwise center of the pattern is placed exactly on a lengthwise or warp thread of the material.

Cut both sides of the garment on the same grain of the cloth and have them correspond exactly.

Provide a seam allowance that is in keeping with the materials. Soft or wiry cloth requires a wider seam than firm fabrics, and woolen or linen, a wider seam than cotton or silk.

IN PREPARING a garment for fitting, we should baste when necessary, but we must baste with a definite purpose, either to determine exactly how the garment will fit or to insure a smooth turn or a perfect seam.

We must respect our cloth, no matter how cheap it is, enough to have our sewing machine in shape to make good stitches. Pulled, puckered stitching lines or oil-soaked thread never does justice to any garment and is always a vexation.

IN FITTING, we must strive to have the garment properly adjusted on the figure —up well at the back of the neck and shoulder seams and entirely in proper position before any changes are made. Sometimes changes seem necessary when the trouble really lies in not having the garment correctly adjusted.

We should remember, too, in fitting, that the shoulder of the human figure curves down slightly between the neck and the shoulder point and that the shoulder seam should lie close to the shoulder; that is, it should never extend on a straight line from the neck to the shoulder point, but, rather, should curve like the figure. A good rule, then, is to fit the shoulder smoothly, baste, stitch, and press carefully, and clip the seam in several places so that it will be perfectly flat.

The armhole seam should always be turned inside the armhole of the blouse, dress, or coat and pressed carefully. Nothing bespeaks the amateur so much as a seam allowed to extend out in the sleeve. The seam makes the sleeve appear heavy in proportion to the body of the garment, which needs this strength because it is larger.

IN FITTING the armhole, we must take care that the shoulder line is not too long to be draggly, nor so long as to make the shoulder appear heavy. Wide shoulders suggest mannish costumes and should be avoided if possible in dresses of dainty or soft fabrics.

In fitting the shoulder line short—that is, well up on the top of the shoulder—we must remember that the upper part of the sleeve will need to be a trifle longer and narrower than when a longer shoulder is used. A comparison of the top of the one-piece, close-fitting sleeve with the mannish sleeve will make this point entirely clear.

In fitting sleeves close, we should bear in mind that they need to be longer than fuller sleeves; also, that smart wrist lines are necessary because they are more conspicuous in close sleeves than in the fuller ones.

TIGHT, stiff inside belts should not be used. They will never allow smart waist-line effects; and just remember that the day of extremely tight waist lines is away, away in the past.

The width of skirts is also a grave consideration. Some think if they have the material there they must use it all, even though it will make the skirt so full as to be conspicuous. And, again, some follow the other extreme, and in their efforts to have a smart skirt they fit it so narrow that they cannot sit down or walk in it with comfort.

After a hem is turned, we should remember always to pin the waist line and also the side seams of the skirt together evenly, and then to lay the skirt out on the table and even up the edge, working from the turned edge so that a smooth, flat hem is acquired. An uneven hem will not make a perfect one, no matter how carefully it is pressed and sewed.

Continued on page 12

Our *Busy* Instruction Department

By SARA L. BYRNE
Department of Instruction

A SUGGESTION came to me from our Editor to write an article on the work of our Instruction Department. I remember that about two years ago I contributed something on practically this same subject, and at first I thought any ideas I might set forth now would be only a repetition of the ones I expressed then. This need not be true, however, for we have grown to such an extent in the past two years that in outward appearance our Instruction Department of today scarcely resembles that of two years ago.

JUST let me take you, as you step from the elevator, into our Instruction Department. First you encounter a large group of workers who are especially trained to handle the first lessons of the Dressmaking Courses—the Essential Stitches and Seams.

You students who have sent us reports on these lessons need no explanation as to how they are handled. We feel that your first reports need especial care, for we are eager to give the greatest possible help on these first stitches and seams, which are so important to your later success in constructing garments. When one of your first lessons is received by us, the answers are carefully checked to see that you have gained just the right idea of the text and then each sampler is gone over separately and with great care. Sometimes we find that an incorrect method has been followed in making the stitch, while sometimes the method is in general correct, but some suggestion may be added to make the work easier or to enable you to obtain more attractive results. In either case, this sampler is returned to you with a comment and if necessary one of our correct samplers accompanies it, to show just how the work should be done.

OF COURSE, we are always working under Mrs. Picken's guidance. Special problems that come up are taken to her for personal attention, and in all our work, each Instructor's highest aim is to follow Mrs. Picken's policy of giving the best that is in her to our work—to consider even the

smallest details worth while if they will help you to master any part of the subject which you are studying.

OUR visitors are always greatly interested in the handling of the lessons on Essential Stitches and Seams, because here, right at the very beginning, we can show how it is possible to teach domestic art by correspondence. Even the most skeptical are convinced that something can be accomplished after they have seen the work that

One Corner of Our Instruction Department

comes to us on these first lessons and have been shown how each report is handled.

In this first large room are also located our Millinery and Cookery Departments, and the work here is equally interesting, the same methods being applied as those used in our dressmaking work.

IN OUR next two rooms are located several groups of Dressmaking Instructors. Each of these has its own particular group of students. When lessons are received in our mailing room they are sorted and sent to the proper group, which is responsible for the progress of its own students.

Each Instructor has been trained to handle the particular kind of lessons assigned to her. Some are very expert in handling the Picken Square, and you will find these at our drafting tables measuring up the drafts that you send us.

Drafting seems such a complicated part of the work *before one has studied it.* But you who have mastered the making of the

foundation waist draft know that the difficulties disappear very quickly when you learn from your Instruction Paper just how and where to locate each point and each line on the draft. Then when your draft comes to us, it is measured very carefully and if any errors are found, these are pointed out to you by means of blue-pencil corrections and comments on the draft.

THEN after you have completed the foundation lessons in Essential Stitches and Seams and Pattern Drafting, you are ready to take up the actual construction of garments—and this, of course, is what you have been looking forward to since you first decided upon this course of study. What a satisfaction it is to us to hear from you: "I have just completed my first waist made according to your instructions. It fits fine and I have received many compliments on my work."

After this come instructions for making various other garments, for embroidering them so they will be more attractive and distinctive; and then comes that interesting paper on "Harmony of Dress." We are delighted when your report shows a thorough understanding of this lesson, because its value can scarcely be estimated.

In fact from the receipt of your first lesson, your progress is closely watched, and I can scarcely express the joy we feel when we receive your Final Examination and it shows that you have profited by our instruction throughout the course.

WE ARE showing you in the illustration one corner of the Instruction Department. I wish you might see it all, and that you might see in reality the many happy faces that are here. A spirit of sincere helpfulness pervades our offices, and, of course, where this exists there cannot fail to be happiness.

We are looking forward to receiving a great number of lesson reports from you during this coming year, and I am sure that each one will mean that you have come a step nearer your goal—the goal we want to help you to reach.

Because your own strength is unequal to the task, do not assume that it is beyond the powers of man; but if anything is within the powers and province of man, believe that it is within your compass also.—Marcus Antoninus.

Soup-Making *Secrets*

By LAURA MacFARLANE
Editorial Department

IT WAS the coldest day of the season up to that time. All the way home on the car, remarks about the weather could be heard floating back and forth, as is usually the case on the first cold or hot day. Some persons were happy about it, and others, of course, were very much annoyed. But the remark that appealed to me most came from a high-school girl who evidently attended one of the downtown schools. In the midst of a discussion about the merits of the high-school play that had been presented a few days before, she burst out with, "Gee, I hope mother has soup tonight. I just love good hot soup on a night like this, don't you, Frances?"

When I stopped to think it over, I realized that she was right. On hot, sultry days, ice cream, ices, and similar dainties are the only things that appeal to us, but when the mercury is hovering around the zero mark, nothing seems "to touch the spot" like a bowl of steaming, appetizing soup. So this month I decided to discuss with you some of the secrets of successful soups, so that if that high-school girl were yours, she would not be disappointed when she returned "hungry as a hound" at the end of her strenuous day.

WITHOUT doubt, the soup course of a meal is neglected oftener than any other. Many housewives omit soup altogether from their meals because they think it either a trouble to make or too expensive a dish, while others give little thought to the making of it and consequently serve an insipid concoction that naturally fails to arouse any enthusiasm among the members of their families. Such conditions are indeed unfortunate, for soup has its place in the meal, in that it stimulates the appetite and aids in the flow of the digestive juices. And appetizing soup is not at all difficult to make if one just understands the underlying principles and applies them properly. In addition, soup is often a real economy, for in it can be utilized materials that might otherwise be wasted.

IF ONE intends to serve soup often, a stock pot made of either enamel or earthenware should be procured. Here should be put the bones from the cooked roast, the trimmings cut from it before it was put into the oven, the tough ends and bones of beefsteak, the carcasses of fowls, together with any remains of stuffing and tough or left-over bits of meat, left-over vegetables, any gravy or unsweetened sauces used for meats and vegetables, the water in which rice, macaroni, or certain vegetables have been cooked, and so on. Great care should be exercised, however, to keep the stock pot scrupulously clean, for nothing is more undesirable than a utensil of this kind if proper attention is not given to it. Frequently it should be emptied, thoroughly washed, and then exposed to the air to dry.

SHOULD meat be purchased expressly for soup making, the tough cuts, such as the shin, the shank, the lower part of the round, the neck, the flank, the shoulder, the tail, and the brisket, are preferable to the tender ones. As far as vegetables are concerned, those which provide the most flavor should be selected, and these include cabbage, cauliflower, asparagus, corn, onions, turnips, carrots, parsnips, tomatoes, beans, peas, lentils, salsify, potatoes, spinach, celery, mushrooms, and okra.

The flavoring of the stock is an extremely important part of soupmaking. Cloves, peppercorns, red, black, and white pepper, paprika, bay leaf, sage, marjoram, thyme, summer savory, tarragon, celery seed, fennel, mint, and rosemary are the flavorings most desired. In addition, Worcestershire sauce is a very valuable flavoring, and celery, parsley, and onions are much used. However, the housewife whose larder will not produce all these things need not feel that she cannot make soups that call for them, for very often certain flavorings may be omitted without any appreciable difference, or something that is on hand may be substituted.

AS A greasy soup is always unpalatable, an effort should be made to remove as much of the grease from it as possible. If the soup is hot, a large part of the grease may be skimmed off with a spoon and the rest then removed with clean blotting paper, tissue paper, or absorbent cotton. If the soup is allowed to become cold, the fat, which collects on top, will harden and it can then be removed by merely lifting off the cake that forms.

THE foundation of the majority of soups is known as stock. Every one who aspires to the making of appetizing soups should therefore be familiar with several kinds of stock. A stock that is suitable for clear soups or bouillon has beef for its basis, is flavored with such flavorings as onion, cloves, peppercorns, parsley, celery and bay leaves, and contains the usual flavorings, salt and pepper. A somewhat more economical stock, called household stock, is made from merely the trimmings of fresh meat, bones, and tough pieces from roasts, steaks, etc. Then there is white stock, which is made from veal and fowl and seasoned with onion, celery, and mace, and which is used for soups that you wish to be particularly dainty and delicious. Any trouble you may encounter in the making of these stocks will be completely overshadowed by the delights experienced when you serve Julienne, noodle, vegetable, and similar soups, for all of these are an easy matter after the stock is prepared.

SOME time ago, I attended a luncheon at which such delicious cream-of-tomato soup was served that the memory of it still lingers with me. Soup of this kind, and in fact all cream soups, can be so easily made that no one needs to forego the pleasure of starting a meal with one of them. They consist merely of a thin white sauce which is properly seasoned and to which are added such vegetables as potatoes, corn, asparagus, peas, onions, or tomatoes in the form of purée or cut into small pieces. And in addition to being most appetizing, these soups have the advantage of being high in food value.

AS IS well known, chowders are soups that have sea food for their basis. Clam chowder is probably the most popular soup of this kind, but if clams are offensive, a fish chowder of any preferred variety of fish may be made. Sometimes, too, certain vegetable mixtures in which milk is used as the liquid are classified as chowders, and these really make a very good substitute when it is impossible to procure sea food. In real chowders, a variety of vegetables may be used, such as onions, potatoes, tomatoes, carrots, and celery, depending on the family's preference and the larder's possibilities.

THE garnishes and accompaniments of soups should not be slighted, either, for they greatly enhance what might otherwise be an unattractive course. Their chief requirement is that they be a contrast to the soup in both consistency and color. Radishes, olives, and celery are the usual garnishes, while crisp wafers, bread sticks, croutons, pastry strips, soup fritters, and forcemeat balls form a group of accompaniments from which selection can be made. In addition, a spoonful or two of whipped cream into which a little mashed pimiento has been stirred added to each dish of soup just before it is brought to the table produces just the touch that many soups need.

But whether a soup is garnished or not, one thing that should never be forgotten concerning it is that, if it is intended to be hot, it should be *hot* when it is served.

Rompers in *Fascinating* Variety

By ALWILDA FELLOWS

Department of Dressmaking

SPRING sewing is bound to have a fascinating aspect when looked at from the romper point of view, for when a romper suit for a wee lad or lassie who is the pride of the household is the point in question, sewing most certainly cannot assume a foreboding nature.

As with every other kind of garment, it is possible to purchase ready-made rompers that will serve the purpose and perhaps be within a reasonable price. But when you are buying rompers for the dearest little one in perhaps the whole wide world, isn't there always a temptation to seek out the very distinctive styles, and then are you not disappointed because you find that their cost is considerably beyond the amount you feel you should pay for them?

Distinctiveness in rompers seems to be dependent on the proper selection of material, alertness to style aspect (this even in regard to rompers), pleasing and unusual combinations of colors, and deft hand touches, all of which are within easy reach of the home sewer, for they may be gained by discriminating observation. Besides, rompers made at home are bound to be inexpensive in their initial cost, and even more so when considered in relation to the wearing qualities of durable, fast-dyed materials, which should almost invariably be selected for home sewing and then carefully shrunk before they are made up.

IN making rompers, even though you feel that you must rely on special patterns for every variation in cut, you may supply a great deal of individuality by varying the material, trimming, and sleeve and neck finishes. A point that you will do well to consider in regard to every romper pattern is whether the length is sufficient from the neck to the division for the leg portions, for if rompers are cut with this measurement too short, it is almost impossible to apply a satisfactory remedy in the fitting.

Some mothers are reluctant to provide dark-colored rompers for their wee folk, because they consider that such colors detract from the children's babyish appearance. In rompers made of two fabrics, the objection to the use of a dark color may be overcome by using it merely in the trousers or lower portion and making the waist of white or of a light color.

Such a plan is followed in the little romper suit at the left in the illustration, but here the trousers are extended over the shoulders in suspender fashion, which lifts them quite out of the ordinary. Sea-green chambray or

linen makes a realistic background for the sail boats that apparently skim over the embroidered billows for the amusement of the diminutive wearer.

The making and trimming of a little suit

such as this require but little skill and time, for the edges are simply finished with darning-stitches worked in black mercerized floss, and the sail boats are merely white scraps of material appliquéd and the design completed with the black floss. The plain blouse of white cotton poplin or dimity is relieved with a touch of the black, which is applied in blanket-stitching over the edges. McCall pattern 2765 is very similar to this design.

IT seems that plaids were made just to grow up with girls, for from the time tiny maids step into their first pair of rompers until they become staid matrons they are permitted to indulge in plaids to their heart's content; first, in only the smallest of plaids, to be sure, but, later, in plaids that correspond in size with their added stature. Little plaids for little girls and big plaids for big girls is a safe rule to follow, for the size of the plaid should never make its wearer appear very small by comparison.

The discreet and novel use of plaid adds much to the charm of the second little romper design, with its full-skirted leg portions and short kimono sleeves stamping it further as distinctly feminine.

Blue-and-white or pink-and-white plaid provides the straight-cut bloomer portions and the bias facings that finish the waist line, sleeves, and neck line, and chambray or gingham of a matching color, the waist and the pocket-trimming pieces.

Woman's Home Companion pattern C4182, which provides for a drop-seat finish, is almost an exact duplicate of this style.

'TWIXT the very languid state of being an infant and the very strenuous times of kindergarten days, it is one's privilege to wear such cunning costumes as that in the center. An old-fashioned flower garden must have inspired the design of the printed sateen, in which yellow predominates. Cretonne or a printed cotton of lighter weight might be preferred for mid-summer wear. In any event, the plain material used for the round yoke and the pockets should harmonize in texture with the figured fabric.

For cutting rompers of this style, you will find McCall pattern 2793 very satisfactory.

BRAID that boasts Mother Goose or animal characters in its design provides an easily applied and interesting trimming for the rompers of a sturdy tan cotton in rep weave shown at the upper right. The design, the material, and the color, all lend to this little costume an air that is decidedly masculine.

If you have difficulty in obtaining braid of the kind you desire for trimming you might substitute a simple embroidery design, or bind the collar and sleeves with a contrasting color and apply wider bands of self-material at each side of the front, or omit the bands entirely.

The lines of Pictorial Review pattern 1350 are practically the same as this design.

WHAT anticipation tinged with excitement accompanies the planning of rompers for that roguish little person who simply will not "stay put!" For just such busybodies, as well as for a somewhat older child, the rompers shown at the extreme right are ideal. These are the same in design as Woman's Home Companion pattern C4131, the front portion being extended between the leg portions to form a flap that buttons over the back.

As illustrated, the rompers are made of orchid cotton crêpe, with smocking in a deeper shade of orchid, self-bindings, and quaint chick designs for patch pockets.

In many cases, a few hand touches, as previously mentioned, add a pleasing individuality to rompers which cannot be attained in any other way. But do not make the mistake of wasting hand work, for, in most instances, machine sewing may be employed with equally or even more satisfactory results. Learn the full value of your sewing-machine attachments and you will find it possible to save much time and patience, besides adding to the rompers the virtues of the ready-made ones with none of their drawbacks.

(Concluded from Page Three)

IN FINISHING a hem—that is, if it is to be decorated by stitching, braid, tucks, or embroidery—the work must be well done because of the prominence of the hem. The hem that is used most is the invisible one. Such a hem, to evidence good workmanship, should have a well-turned edge and stitches that do not show on the right side; also, the finished hem should be thoroughly and carefully pressed from the right side, but a cloth should always be placed over the material before the iron is applied.

To make hemming-stitches that will not show on the right side, hold the hem edge from you and slip-stitch the skirt to the hem with loose, easy stitches. Never make tight hemming-stitches.

In putting on braid of any kind, hold it easy but never tight or full, and always have the material to which it is to be applied laid out smooth, so that the braid may be attached smoothly.

A READY-TO-WEAR manufacturer once said that he used only a few fasteners on the garments he made so as to avoid the danger of a compact, heavy appearance when the dress was fastened. In the last fitting, we should determine just where fasteners are needed, marking with pins. Perhaps six fasteners will be sufficient to hold the garment together. Many new dressmakers are careless about fasteners, sometimes allowing the stitches to show through on the right side. This is always a grievous error.

FOR embroidery work, an important point is to select a design that is neither common nor patchy, and especially one that can be done skilfully; also, one that is not too elaborate for one's time or needs. Use a color, weight, and texture that is entirely in harmony with the material or agreeably contrasts with it. Make the stitches loose enough so that they cannot possibly draw, and then press them carefully from the wrong side, using a well-padded board and gentle, even pressure.

Woman's Institute *Question Box*

Variety in Apron Trimmings

For my children I find the Mother Goose style of apron very practical. Oftentimes such an apron may be used to protect a school frock after study hours are over, thus making it unnecessary to remove the little dress in order to keep it fresh for the next day. But I believe my chief reason for considering this apron a "stand-by" is because it may serve as a substitute for a bib at mealtime. You know, most children when they begin to follow a great many grown folks' customs insist upon discarding bibs and using napkins as mother and father do. If I make the little aprons sufficiently attractive, my children, instead of being hesitant about wearing them at the table, are very proud of them and seem to forget all about napkins.

Now, this is the reason I am writing for your assistance—my ideas for trimming are exhausted. Can you furnish a new supply?   J. McA.

How much better it is to try to make your children's duties a pleasure rather than a trial for them!

You failed to mention the kinds of trimming that you have employed, but from the following you may gain some new ideas: Animals or Mother Goose characters seem to be the most interesting trimming. A variety of very attractive stamping designs may be obtained from any of the well-known pattern agencies, such as Pictorial Review, Butterick, and McCall's. These may be embroidered in a contrasting color or cut out of material of contrasting color and appliquéd in position.

The most recent issue of the *Children's Costume Royal* gave patterns for large animal figures—rabbits, elephants, etc.—that might be used as pockets, these being placed at each side of the apron facing each other and the sides and lower portion of the design appliquéd, with the upper edge finished free from the apron. For appliquéing you might use either mercerized floss or yarn; simple overcasting stitches, blanket or scallop-buttonhole stitches may be employed according to the nature of the material.

Dutch scenes embroidered in white or old blue on rather dark-blue chambray make effective trimming. Embroidered or appliquéd kewpies are also bound to please.

The outer edge of the apron should be finished, in most instances, to correspond with the other trimming. Bindings of contrasting color, facings applied to the right side, or tiny hems finished with featherstitching, cross-stitching, or some embroidery outlining stitch are all suitable.

Want to Get Acquainted?

The following Institute students desire to become acquainted with other Institute students residing in their localities:

Eastern Oregon ....M. B. L.
Cornucopia, Wisconsin ....H. J. E.
Woodstock, Ontario, Canada...............W. B. J.
Binghamton, Port Dickson, or Johnson City,
  New York ....G. R.
Orange, New Jersey ....M. F.
St. Charles, Missouri ....R. U.
Chicago, Illinois ....E. B. O'N.
Albany County or Watervliet, New York....G. S.
Chico, California ....J. M. D.
St. Paul, Minnesota ....E. P.
Nampa, Idaho ....A. M. S.
Idaho ....E. L.
New York City ....M. C.
Toronto, Canada ....J. B.
Englewood, New Jersey ....A. W.
New York City.............................L. L.
United States or Canada...................E. C. T.
Reading, Pennsylvania ....M. M. R.
Washington, New Jersey...............E. H. DeV.
Florida, particularly Jacksonville........R. H. B.
Kansas ....E. H.

I should like to correspond with students taking the Professional Dressmaking and Tailoring Course.   L. V. S.

Is there a student in some good town in Arkansas where I could go in business? I would like very much to sell hats and want to locate in some good town.   A. B. E.

I should like to correspond with any one taking the Dressmaking Course.   I. M. B.

I should like to become acquainted with some American girls who are students of the Institute.   M. R., Arroya, Porto Rico

I should like to correspond or if possible study with some Institute students living in New York City.   Fannie Gersten,
          144 Attorney Street, New York City

I should like to hear from some of the students who are taking the Complete Dressmaking Course at the Institute and who are 18 years old.   G. C.

If other Woman's Institute students would like to get in touch with the inquiring students, we shall be glad to supply the names and addresses.

Altering Back of Waist Pattern

In checking up the measurements of the waist pattern I used in making my guide, I found the length of back too short; the front measurement, however, was correct. To make the back portion sufficiently long, I slashed it crosswise below the bust line and separated the pattern pieces. This, however, made the back under-arm seam shorter than the front under-arm seam. What should I have done in such a case?   E. A. S.

Provided the under-arm seam was of the correct length, you should have graduated the alteration in order to add no length at the under arm. By this I mean that you should have separated the pieces at the center back, but not at the under-arm seam. Generally, when length must be added at the center back, a little extra length is also necessary at the under arm. To provide this, separate the pieces of the back pattern portion the required amount at the center back and at the under arm; also, slash the front portion of the pattern and separate this merely at the under arm.

Length and Width of Skirts

Fashion items are still conflicting in regard to skirt lengths. Will you kindly tell me what length will be considered correct in the spring? Am I correct in assuming that the skirts of spring styles will be somewhat wider?   R. B.

There is no doubt that spring styles will have shorter, wider skirts, yet there is no evidence that the change will be startling. For most figures, the proper skirt length will probably be 7 to 9 inches from the floor. The range in skirt widths will be more decided—1½ to 1¾ yards for heavy materials and 2 yards or more for materials of lighter weight.

Rubber Stamp

For your convenience we have arranged to supply a rubber stamp containing your name, address, and class letters and number. Such a stamp will prove a great convenience, for with it you can give us quickly and legibly the information we need on every lesson report you send us, as well as on every letter or other communication and on every envelope. Also, you can use the stamp to mark the books you own, your laundry, or anything that you wish.

The price of one of these stamps with your name, address, and class letters and number and a self-inking pad is only 60 cents, postpaid.

Fashion Service
— SUPPLEMENT —

Each Issue of *Vintage Notions Monthly* includes a *Fashion Service Supplement*. You will read about the fashion styles popular in the early twentieth century and receive a collectible fashion illustration to print and frame.

The students of the Woman's Institute would also receive a publication called *Fashion Service*. Where the *Inspiration* newsletter instructed them on all aspects of the domestic arts, not only sewing but also cooking, housekeeping, decorating, etc., *Fashion Service* was devoted entirely to giving current fashions with a key to their development.

Fashion Service prided itself on providing it's readers with reliable style information and the newest fashion forecasting. The publication wasn't just eye candy. The Institute stressed the importance of studying the fashions to benefit the sewer's understanding of dressmaking. To quote founder Mary Brooks Picken, "Once the principles of design...and of construction... are understood, beautiful garments will result. This publication comes to you as an aid to this desired goal. Read the text of every page and reason out the why of every illustration and description that your comprehension of designing and construction may be enlarged and your appreciation made more acute."

Today, these articles and illustrations give us a historically accurate view of what fashion really meant 100 years ago. Not only can we study these articles for an "of-the-time" style snapshot, but just as their students did, we can also learn to understand the principles of design and increase our sewing skills. In each issue, look for a collectible illustration in the back of the supplement!

"I want every Institute Student to have a copy of the New Fall and Winter Edition of Fashion Service"
—Mary Brooks Picken

WE ARE hurrying this message to you in order that you may have, with the news of the dedication of our wonderful new home, another bit of news that is vitally important to you in the planning and making of all your new fall clothes.

Fashion Service for Fall and Winter 1921–1922 is ready, and, in the opinion of every one here at the Institute, it is the finest, the most attractive, the most interesting, and the most helpful issue of *Fashion Service* we have published.

The new issue contains 83 fashion figures presenting the best among the new ideas for dresses, wraps, and children's clothes for fall and winter. And each figure is accompanied by detailed description and instruction telling just how to develop the style shown, with suggestions as to the colors and materials that can be used to the best advantage.

You who have had a copy of *Fashion Service* already know better than we can possibly tell you here that the Institute has created for its students a new kind of fashion information. You know that no matter how many fashion magazines you might buy, it is only in *Fashion Service* that you find just the style you want with detailed instruction that makes possible the easy development of the appealing picture into a distinctive, becoming dress or wrap for yourself or your customer.

And so whatever else you may have in the way of style information, you will want your copy of the new *Fashion Service* at once. And we have made it possible for you to have it.

Each Woman's Institute student receives two issues of *Fashion Service* free—afterwards the price is $3 per copy, or $5 per year. If you have received but one issue and your scholarship account is in good standing, you will get the new issue without cost. If you have already had two issues, your subscription has expired.

But we are so anxious for you who have received two copies to have the new issue anyway that we are making a special offer. Send us *only $2* and a copy of the new Fall and Winter Edition will come to you at once; or send us $3 and we will send you the new issue and also enter your subscription for next Spring's issue. So you will receive two issues for the cost of one issue to others.

The new *Fashion Service* will be ready to mail when this reaches you. Every day's delay in getting it deprives you of the most valuable fashion information you can have this fall.

Send your order today—$2 if you want only the issue now ready, $3 for a year's subscription.

Model 26

**Fall and Winter
Fashion Service**

Woman's Institute
Merchandise Service Department
Scranton, Pa.

One-Piece Coat Dress

Style.—Modern corsets have produced youthful figures and made possible beautiful one-piece dresses—dresses that hang from the shoulders and are held in slightly at the waist with a belt modest in its narrowness.

One-piece dresses agree with the three constructive points of harmonious dress: they are artistic; economical as regards material and time to make and to put on; and, in the majority of cases, becoming, especially to the American woman. Such dresses make possible that which is most sought by well-dressed women—simplicity in dress.

Material and Pattern.—Cloth, because of its weight and softness, seems most adaptable as a one-piece dress material. The heavy satins, such as chinchilla satin, are also especially good. Tricotine, fine serge, light-weight broadcloth, and duvetyn are almost invariably beautiful as well as practical for one-piece coat dresses such as those here illustrated. The dress shown in the feature picture, for instance, is developed in soft, midnight-blue, fine-twilled tricotine.

Bands of blue grosgrain ribbon trim the collar, sash, and sleeves, as well as the sides below the waist. Bands of bias self-material embroidered with heavy rope silk of American Beauty color in a short darning-stitch could also be used. Tiny silver buttons placed as shown further emphasize smartness in color selection.

Unless you are definitely skilful in embroidery work, it would be better for you to use the ribbon or brown or black embroidery silk rather than American Beauty as trimming, because these colors will not show irregularities in stitches as will the brighter color. Bias bands of the material lined with a bright color and held in place with buttons are also effective as trimming, especially when very nicely made.

Taffeta with pin tucks ⅜ inch apart is also attractive for bands and offers a trimming variation that is thoroughly satisfactory.

Pictorial Review design No. 9087 provides a good one-piece dress pattern to use for a straight-line dress like that illustrated. This particular pattern opens at the under arm and shoulder, but is easy to arrange so that the opening can come at the center front. An allowance of 3 inches should be made on each side of the center-front line for the double-breasted effect.

Cutting.—In the cutting of this dress, no interlining will have to be provided except a true bias piece of light-weight lawn or cambric for the shawl collar. This inner support will help to keep the collar in shape and balance it with the front. However, if satin or light-weight cloth is used, the interlining should be omitted.

If it is known that a long revers line is becoming, it will be necessary to use a small V vest. This should be put on a foundation lining so that it cannot interfere with the ease in appearance necessary in the front of this type of dress. The vest can be of the same material as the dress and trimmed in the same way, or it can be of appropriate lace or Georgette.

The narrow belts used on tricotine, serge, and Poiret twill dresses are almost always cut on a true bias and measure ⅜ to ¾ inch wide when finished. The twill in this way comes crosswise of the belt and adds to its attractiveness.

Construction and Fitting.—In a one-piece coat dress where the bust is prominent, the side seams may drop down and give a diagonal wrinkle from the center front and center back of the skirt to the side seams. To overcome this, lay a crosswise dart at the waist line, beginning at the side seam and carrying the dart out to nothing toward the center front and center back.

In placing the dart, take up enough material so that the skirt portion will hang smoothly—that is, with a straight grain of material—around the lower edge and through the hips. If the material of the dress is heavy, baste the dart on the wrong side and make a plain seam; then trim away any unnecessary material and press the seam open.

In some dresses, especially satin, a smart line is often obtained by making this dart alteration 2 to 4 inches below the waist line and finishing it with a tiny tuck or tiny corded piping. In many of the commercial patterns, the dart line is provided in the pattern and made to serve as a trimming feature.

Short, narrow shoulders, where set-in sleeves are used, are the rule at present. Fit your shoulders easily and smoothly, and remember, in basting, to hold the front shoulder seam close and the back easy, so that a good effect will result. Baste and stitch carefully, keeping in mind that any alteration made at the shoulder seam will affect the sleeve unless a corresponding alteration is made there.

If you are inclined to stoutness, hold to set-in sleeves in preference to kimono sleeves, but fit your shoulders narrow and the upper part of your sleeves slightly snug and with the greatest care, for heavy appearing shoulders are rarely necessary and can almost always be overcome by right fitting.

It has frequently been emphasized that the shoulder line, waist line, collar line, and hem finish are the chief style features of a dress and the most important ones to observe. A French designer would put the skirt length before these, asserting that the skirt length tells instantly of the newness of the garment.

While we may not altogether agree with him, the skirt length is of great importance. Although every woman's skirt length is a law unto herself, no woman wants to wear extremely long skirts when the tendency is for definitely short ones, and though we decry skirts very short, we have to admit that they are smart, and especially so when good hose of exactly the right shade for the dress and smart well-kept shoes are worn.

Finishing.—Very plain clothes are the smartest clothes, but to have them beautiful they must be right in line and skilfully made. An apprentice in patterns could make the dress illustrated without any difficulty, but the stitching, pressing, and finishing are telltales in such a plain dress, the hem especially. This should be carefully gathered at the top, its fulness shrunken out, and then bound with a bias binding of silk or with seam binding.

The binding must be put on easily so that the top of the hem cannot draw. After binding, press the hem carefully again and catch it in place with long, medium-loose silk stitches. Remove the basting threads before the hem is firmly pressed, so that the marks from the basting-stitches will not show on the right side. A good point to remember is to fasten the hem turn just enough to hold it to the skirt, rather than try to fasten the skirt to the hem.

To make the narrow belt, pin the right sides of the material together and baste and stitch, using a loose stitch. Trim the seam, press it open, and turn the strip right side out. Then press carefully, making sure to have the seam come in the center of one side of the belt.

Press the armhole seam in toward the waist, so as to emphasize that the sleeve is always set into the waist and not the waist into the sleeve. Remember that fine gathering-stitches in the top of the sleeve help greatly in adjusting the fulness so that not a wrinkle is evident. If you use care in basting, fitting, pressing, and stitching the plain, open seams of the shoulder and under arm and in applying the shawl collar and facing, following generally the instructions in the lesson entitled *Tailored Suits, Coats, and Capes,* great satisfaction will result in developing this coat dress.

Model 1

Variations of One-Piece Coat Dress

In designing a dress, do not consider lines alone, but give full value to color and texture; then suit all three to your individual requirements, thus insuring distinctive and becoming dress. The plain fabrics that dominate this season require great care in handling, so that the lines will be rightly placed to prove both interesting and becoming. Plain fabrics always demand subdued color. The very soft fabrics permit more definite colors than do the firm fabrics; but there are few types that can wear definite colors even when the fabric does lend its aid. This is proved by the popularity of the ever-becoming blue cloth of serge, tricotine, and twill.

Model 1A.—Navy, fine-twill serge uses old-blue or deep-turquoise and silver embroidery for its trimming in this model. The collar is cut straight at the center back and almost a true bias at the front, and is made of only one thickness of material.

The binding of the collar, sleeves, and skirt is of ½-inch blue grosgrain ribbon. This makes a neat, attractive binding that is secure enough to be practical and yet dainty and pleasing for a dress of this type. Before the binding is applied, the edge of the material should be carefully overcasted with buttonhole or No. 40 cotton thread to secure it from raveling or pulling out when the narrow ribbon binding is in place.

The fronts of this model are cut full length. To do this, place the selvages together and open the material out full width. This makes it possible to cut the skirt part in two pieces, that is, without side seams, but brings a seam at the waist line across the back. This joining should be made with just a plain, open seam. Seams such as this must always be carefully basted, stitched, and pressed to insure their lying perfectly flat. As a rule, the seam edges of such joinings are overcasted or notched rather than bound, in order to avoid bulk.

This model shows the side alteration placed 1½ inches below the waist line and used as a trimming feature, as previously explained.

Tunics are frequently favored for one-piece dresses. Many times the dress is merely made shorter and a foundation skirt provided with its lower part of the dress material and its upper part of appropriate lining fabric. If a long skirt is known to be more becoming, use it and provide a tunic effect in the dress to get the short-skirt effect.

Model 1B.—Though slightly extreme in its simplicity, this model is an unusually becoming type of dress, especially for a well-poised figure. The military-flare collar is a feature necessary to emphasize the dignity of the straight center-front line.

The original of this model is of midnight-blue tricotine with rust, or cauldron, duvetyn as trimming, this being a new shade of dull red with a brownish hue. This trimming is blended into the dress material with dark-blue silk floss and dull-gold embroidery applied with the darning-stitch in zigzag outline.

Model 1C.—In this model, rust duvetyn is enhanced with dull-silver embroidery. Luxurious material and good embroidery work are the two essential features of this dress. A heavy Poiret twill, serge, or tricotine would develop nicely in this type. Blue cloth with brown, dark-blue, dark-red, or dull-gold embroidery would be very attractive.

A plain one-piece dress pattern opening under the arm is right for this dress, a long sleeve being appropriate because of the heavy embroidery through the body of the dress. The sash tying at the left side of the back is also a feature to consider, for coming at this place it is unusually smart in style and does not interfere with the embroidery line at the front.

If the collar line is developed as illustrated, a piece of muslin should be used in shaping the back collar, so as to get the width and position right for the individual. In finishing the neck, use two rows of darning-stitches close together all around the back-collar portion and the front-neck edge.

Model 1D.—This model boasts of three definite style features: the collar with its Robespierre flare, the Oriental band at the center front, and the modified peg-top pocket hip. In dark or seal brown, with facings of pheasant and a pheasant band embroidered in dark brown, this dress proves decidedly pleasing. Midnight-blue tricotine with black satin or crêpe meteor facing and a black band embroidered in American Beauty and dull gold also makes a smart color combination.

Pictorial Review pattern No. 9087 serves splendidly as a foundation pattern for this type of dress. The make-believe peg pockets should be pinned in place, carefully shaped, as illustrated, and then bound with narrow ribbon or a true bias satin binding.

The pockets may be faced with a material to match the collar and band, but not if the color is definitely conspicuous, as it will give too much color for such a prominent place in the dress.

The size of the band at the center front depends on the size of the individual and the color used. A band of contrasting color should be smaller than one of blending or self-color. A band 18 or 20 inches in length and 2⅜ to 3½ inches in width will be right in most instances.

Model 1E.—To have a lithesome figure is the desire of most women, and Model 1E is just the kind to make one wish for such a figure. At first glance, one would feel certain that only a slender type could wear such a dress well, but a plump figure could also wear it, especially if the waist line were inclined in the least to suppleness.

The original of this dress is in sparrow color, which is light dull brown, with vest, collar, and embroidery of light-almond color, which is three or four shades lighter than sparrow. Little flecks of radio-blue and dull-gold embroidery are used with the almond floss to add life and smartness to the color combination.

The waist-line cord is of heavy sparrow-colored silk. Usually this can be purchased by the yard and the ends then finished with tassels, a 2½-yard length being the amount needed for the average sash. A smaller silk cord may be plaited together if a cord of proper size is not available.

Use a plain one-piece pattern, sewing the side seams and the under arms together and thus finishing the dress in slip-over effect. The center panel comes up over the guimpe and serves as a gate to admit the figure. It is then secured by fasteners at the neck when the dress is on.

The front skirt panel is merely an apron of self-material cut and finished to come about 4 inches to the front of each side seam and 2 inches above the skirt's lower edge. The position of the apron below the waist line should be determined in fitting so as to insure individual becomingness, for the location of every sash or waist-line finish is an individual matter. As the sash in this instance must conceal the outer edge of the apron panel, the position of the two must agree. The top of the apron is turned under and stitched directly on the edge in a most inconspicuous way.

The guimpe in this case is cut over a plain-foundation waist pattern and made to serve both as a guimpe and a foundation lining for the dress. It opens in the center front and its neck line is finished with a Dutch collar, while its lower edge comes about 4 inches above the waist line, this being finished in a plain ¼-inch hem. Pussy-willow silk, crêpe de Chine, Georgette, or fine batiste may be selected for the guimpe and collar. If desired, the same material may be placed under the sleeve openings, slip-stitched at the upper edge, and caught in place with inconspicuous stitches at the cuff edge.

1E

1B

1A

1D

1C

Long-Tunic Dress

Style.—The best dressed woman of any social class studies her own dress possibilities. She knows what the dress manufacturers have to offer in fabrics. She not only observes but reads about the fashions in reliable fashion magazines and newspapers.

Keeping up with the changing fashions and studying them intelligently is the rational economical attitude toward dress. Therefore, keep up with fashions; don't wait until you feel that you have to accept them. Study them as they come and interpret them for your own individual needs; then your costumes will reflect the mode and yet express that distinction in dress always so much admired and so eagerly sought.

Take the long-tunic dress as an example of intelligent dress. Who would want to wear a uniform dress, so much advocated, when a style with as much individuality and genuine smartness as are evident in this dress is available?

To hear an artist talk of art, color, and line and their adaptation to individuals, one feels appalled. The responsibility of dressing in good taste and becomingly seems tremendous, yet the elimination of unbecoming colors and lines and a continued striving for the right expression of individuality will unquestionably gain their reward in improvement equal to the comprehension, earnestness, and persistence evidenced.

Material and Pattern.—Moccasin-brown silk duvetyn or satin, Hindu brown, or Arctic blue cloth, or even the reliable blue serge would prove splendidly appropriate for a dress of this type. For the average figure, 6¼ yards of 40-inch material or 5 yards of 54-inch material is needed, unless a sham skirt is used underneath the tunic; then the amounts may be reduced 1¼ to 1½ yards.

In order to insure smartness and a well-fitted effect in a one-piece dress, a muslin model is almost a necessity, for if a very decided change must be made in fitting the upper part of the dress, an even more decided change than can be taken care of with an ordinary seam allowance is often necessary in the skirt lines. Such changes may be accomplished in the muslin model by means of piecings and the new seam lines then marked so that they may be followed in cutting the dress material.

Use a plain one-piece dress pattern as a guide in cutting the muslin model for this dress. Provide the extension that is necessary at the center front, mark the dart line above the hip line of the pattern and parallel with it, and slash and separate the portion of the pattern below this line to provide fulness. Then, instead of cutting a curved line, like the pattern, from the center front to the side seam, leave the lower edge straight. The extra length may be taken up in the dart and cut away, thus permitting the hem to be turned on a straight grain of the material.

Outline the back panel to make it of a becoming width, and provide a 1½-inch seam allowance on both of its edges, as well as on the side back edges to which it is joined. Also, provide a seam line with fulness gathered into it, to be made an extension of the dart in the front portion. Provide an allowance of about 2½ inches for finishing the lengthwise edges of the front opening.

In fitting the muslin model, consider the sleeves. Long or short sleeves may be used satisfactorily in this model. Also, decide on the amount of overlap of the front and the fulness of the tunic, especially at the sides just below the waist. In the case of cloth, the tunic should be ⅝ to ⅞ yard fuller than the foundation skirt, counting the overlap at the center front. For satin, the tunic should measure ¾ to 1 yard more than the underskirt. This fulness will not seem so great when its bulk is concealed in the plaits of the back panel and in the overlap of the front.

Before removing the muslin model, form a muslin collar pattern and, as in the Tuxedo-scarf dress, make the lengthwise threads of the collar parallel with those in the waist at the front and form a bias seam in the center back of the collar.

Construction.—Gather the fulness of the front dart and the back horizontal seam line, using very small stitches, and distribute the gathers evenly in basting them to the turned lower edge of the waist. The gathered portion is quite conspicuous and unless the fulness is carefully adjusted, this detail will detract from the general attractiveness of the design.

When the gathers are basted in position, baste the under-arm, shoulder, side-back, and sleeve seams, and turn under the back-panel edges and baste the panel flat to the dress. Also, turn back the allowance made for the finish of the lengthwise front edges. Then baste the seams of the foundation skirt, leaving the left seam open at the top for a placket finish.

Fitting.—Place the foundation skirt on the figure and make any changes in this that may be necessary. Then put on the tunic dress and observe every detail usually considered in the fitting of a dress of this kind. If the muslin model used for the dress pattern was fitted properly, few, if any, changes will be necessary in this fitting. In order to make sure that the armhole curve is correct, turn under the allowance made on the armhole edge of the waist and pin the sleeve in position. Much of the smartness of a tailored dress is dependent on the fitting of the sleeve and of the armhole curve; therefore, these points must not be passed over lightly.

With this done, mark the position for the buttons. Two large buttons are sufficient for a style of this kind.

Finishing.—Finish the dart and the corresponding seam line in the back with a row of stitching placed very close to the turned lower edge of the waist. Finish the foundation-skirt seams and the shoulder, under-arm, and sleeve seams of the overdress as plain pressed-open seams and either overcast or bind them. Stitch the edges of the back panel about 1-inch outside of the seam line, in order to produce a soft plait, which may be merely pressed in position. Stitch the armhole as a plain seam; then turn the edges in toward the body portion of the waist and finish them together. Either overcast or bind the inside edge of the allowance made at the center front, but do not hem this edge to the dress. Instead, secure it in position at the upper end with the collar facing, which is extended to the turned lengthwise edge of the front, and secure the lower end of the allowance in the skirt hem. Such a finish will produce a more desirable effect at the front than if an attempt is made to secure the front hem its entire length.

Finish the lower edge of the sleeves with a bias ¼-inch finished binding or with narrow braid binding, whichever you prefer. Make the girdle of a double bias strip, which, when finished, is about 1 inch wide and 2 yards long. Then, finish the placket in the foundation skirt and turn the hems in both the foundation and outer skirts, and while the dress is on the figure tack the girdle in position. Remove the dress and secure the skirt hems with fine, loose hemming-stitches.

To make the buttons, cover molds about 1¼ inches in diameter with self-material. Buttons are frequently decorated with embroidery-stitches sometimes in a deeper or a lighter color, especially when large buttons are used, as in this case. Decorated buttons may be purchased if the material is very luxurious. Some of the buttons to be had this season are attractive enough to serve as brooches. Make the loops of self-covered cord, provided you have bound the collar and sleeves with self-material; but if you have used bindings of braid, make the loops by folding braid over the cord and whipping the edges together closely.

Model 5

Variations of Long-Tunic Dress

Model 5A.—This design insists on spelling the one word artistic, and it seems right that it should, for it is so thoroughly practical, so definitely useful, and evidences simplicity in every line. Perhaps the artistic emphasis rests on the ever-favored panels. At any rate, the dress conforms to three rules of art —usefulness, simplicity, and appropriateness. Consequently, it lends itself to the needs of many; at the same time, it is desirable for many kinds of materials and especially where two materials are to be used in combination, a point often desired for dresses of cloth and silk. In this dress, for instance, if the contrasting material is used for inserted strips rather than for an entire underskirt, with 1¾ yards of 40-inch satin and an out-of-fashion cloth suit or dress, a new dress can be created, and if the workmanship is skilfully done there need not appear even a suspicion of made-overness.

Crêpe de Chine, that well-known fabric which has proved its reliability and usefulness by its return to decided favor, is combined with duvetyn for this particular model, two very lovely shades of tan being used, one comparatively light and the other quite deep. The odd embroidered border that emphasizes the lower edge of the duvetyn bodice is developed of wool floss in a color that matches the deeper shade of tan crêpe de Chine.

For the average figure, provide 2 yards of 54-inch material and 2¾ yards of contrasting material 40 inches wide if you wish to make an entire underskirt, or merely 1¾ yards if, instead, you prefer to use the contrasting fabric for inserted strips in the skirt.

Attach the skirt and vest for this dress to the lining and finish the overblouse separately, with a ¼-inch bias binding of crêpe de Chine at the extreme lower edge. Then, to hold the blouse together at a point in line with the buttons, sew on a large hook and eye and apply the buttons merely for decoration.

In finishing the lower edge of the skirt, make a hem in the foundation, but face the loose, or "flying," panels.

Model 5B.—This slip-over dress, with its short sleeves and low neck, does not, at first thought, seem just right for a dress for fall and winter, although there are many short sleeves this season, even in dresses of very heavy fabrics. But, with the first whisper of winter, furs are donned, so that the low neck does not matter greatly, and there seems to be a pair of long gloves right in length, color, and texture for every pair of short sleeves.

Long-tunic dresses are naturally forerunners of wider skirts, and when the tunic has as much fulness as is provided by the plaits of this model and is made so long that the foundation skirt is hardly evident, one requires but little imagination to picture the skirts of styles that we may have another season. Foundation skirts, because of the manner in which they are covered, are bound to realize their insignificance sooner or later and take their place in the background until they are called again for use with the shorter tunic.

Model 5B was developed with the inserted panel and the foundation skirt of black satin, with marine-blue tricotine for the overdress. This was embroidered with Burgundy and tan beads in a very unusual conventional rose design.

For developing this dress for the average figure, provide 3⅜ yards of tricotine, 1⅜ yards of satin, and 1⅞ yards of China silk or lining material for a plain foundation slip to which the satin may be attached.

Cut the foundation slip on plain, straight lines and just a trifle lower at the neck line than the outer dress, in order that it will not have a tendency to show when the dress is worn. Make the front skirt portion of the slip of satin, but use a piece of satin only 8 or 10 inches wide to form the back lower edge of the slip. Make the waist portion of the lining entirely of China silk, and insert strips of satin under the slashed openings of the outer waist, arranging for an opening at the left side of the slash so that the dress may be easily slipped over the head.

To make the belt illustrated, use a double bias strip that, when finished, will be 1 inch wide and about 10 inches longer than the loose waist measurement generally followed in making belts and girdles for one-piece dresses. At each end of the bias strip, sew on a large self-covered button and snap fasteners so that the belt may be lapped and easily secured.

Model 5C.—Another slip-over-the-head type of dress, having no opening except at the center front, is seen in this model of medium-gray duvetyn combined with crêpe meteor of a slightly darker shade. The stand-up Dutch collar and the "underneath cuffs" are distinctive features, as are also the three-quarter-around belt and the zigzag embroidery developed in maroon-colored wool. This dress would also prove a real delight if developed in dark blue and black, or brown and tan, in either cloth or silk.

The style is an excellent one for the medium type of person, and with a few slight changes might be adapted to a figure inclined to stoutness. For instance, the tucks in the waist portion might be made to turn in instead of out and the panel effects thus narrowed; the embroidery in crosswise band effect might be dropped to the lower edge of the skirt and attention therefore not concentrated at the waist line; and the collar might be made to fit a V-shaped neck.

For developing this model are required 3¾ yards of duvetyn, ¾ yard of satin, and 3½ yards of China silk for the foundation slip. Make sleeves in the foundation slip in order that the satin band may be attached to them.

Model 5D.—Gleaming jet and spangles and black mirror velvet are all that one could desire in the ideal evening frock for the mature woman; but when one considers them in a gown for a more youthful type, one realizes their inability to provide all the qualities essential for success. And then comes an inspiration that suggests a bodice of crêpe meteor in a rich, lovely color copied exactly from the marigold. Thus is evolved a gown that any young matron would delight in, for the velvet and the arrangement of the drapery signify dignity, while the bright marigold provides just the touch of color necessary to remind one that youth has not entirely departed.

It will be necessary to provide for the development of a dress such as this 3½ yards of velvet and 1¼ yards of crêpe meteor if you wish to make set-in sleeves, or only 1 yard of crêpe meteor if you prefer the kimono type. Also, 1 yard of China silk is required for the upper part of the foundation skirt.

Do not attempt to make this dress without first trying out the drapery in muslin, for it will require considerable experimenting in order to make the drapery assume just the effect that is illustrated. Use a 2½- or 3-yard length of muslin and start arranging it by pinning the end, which is cut on a crosswise grain, so that about ½ yard extends below and the rest above the waist line at the left side back. Then draw the muslin down at the left side and bring it across the front so that it shows but a few inches of the foundation skirt. Pin the muslin at the waist line, laying it in soft plaits to hold the fulness; then loop it down at the right side and up at the back, and arrange the decided drape that is evident at the side. Next, bring the muslin up to the left shoulder, lay it in soft plaits at this point, cut the outline of the back panel, and trim away the surplus material at the waist line. Then extend the muslin across the front of the figure to the right side back and cut a bias waist-line band in one with the drapery, or, if you find it easier, cut the waist-line band separate from the drapery. Do not attempt to shape the lower edge of the drapery; rather, leave this, as it falls, on a lengthwise thread of the fabric.

5C

5B

5D

5A

Straight-Line Dress

Style.—Frequently, women rounded out in body complain that the fashion magazines overlook them, giving few designs entirely suitable for their needs; hence, the straight-line dress in this Fashion Service. It is one that can be developed becomingly for a "partridge plump" or a slightly plump woman, and the reasons for this are to be found in the long vest line, the long embroidered side lines, the front skirt panel, the full-length panel in the back, as well as the diagonal line over the hips. A side plait is used at each panel edge in front and back to give, unnoticeably, fulness for the large figure. Dresses for plump and large women should have the position of every line carefully planned out by means of a muslin model; then the dress itself should always be well made, with smart simplicity or dignified decoration a definite style feature.

If, before deciding on a dress, large women would always try to visualize themselves sitting down in the dress, rather than standing just as erect as they know how, they would obtain a more satisfactory result. Oftentimes dresses are too small through the hips or too tight around the waist or too stiff around the neck, and consequently they slip up on the figure. When they do this, they not only appear uncomfortable but actually are.

Smooth-surface materials are almost invariably in better taste than rough weaves for the large figure, and these materials make possible plaits so carefully placed and pressed as to be almost unnoticeable. Plaits of this kind should be preferred by those who choose to look more slender than they really are.

Ribbonzine embroidery thread, which is very soft and resembles narrow, flat braid, is used for decoration in this straight-line dress. Ribbonzine works up so quickly and so satisfactorily in the heavy materials that it is much appreciated by dress artists. For instance, the darning-stitches in the front, which add much to the attractiveness and value of the dress, can be made in a short time with ribbonzine.

In executing long embroidery lines like this, lay the material out very flat and carefully secure it in place on the table so that the stitches cannot draw in any place as they are being made. One of the chief beauties of good embroidery work is the easy placing of the thread. Not one stitch should be drawn the least bit, for tight stitches never make successful embroidery.

Material and Pattern.—Firm, soft cloth of attractive twill, such as serge, and heavy satins, silk faille, or poplin, and Canton crêpe, all lend themselves admirably to this type of dress. The poplins and crêpes are especially appropriate when made up crosswise of the material so that the heavy thread runs down rather than across or around.

McCall pattern No. 9704 gives to a nicety the pattern lines of this straight-line dress, which is developed in nut-brown duvetyn with copper-colored satin collar and cuffs and embroidery in self-colored ribbonzine with a few silver threads to give it character. For the average figure, 3 yards of 54-inch material and ¼ yard of satin will be sufficient for making this dress.

Cutting.—Place the center-front and center-back edges of the panels on a lengthwise fold of the material, and arrange the other pattern sections so that a lengthwise thread extends through the center of each. An exception to this rule may be made, as already suggested, if you are using corded material, in which case a piecing will be necessary at the back waist line.

If you wish the neck-line finish illustrated here rather than the one provided in the pattern, use a plain front-closing pattern as a guide in cutting the center front and the neck line, and make allowance beyond the center front for a facing about 4 inches wide at the neck edge and 2 inches wide at the waist line.

If you do not desire plaits under the panels, slash the side sections of the skirt pattern and separate them from 2 to 4 inches, thus giving fulness that may be gathered in at the diagonal joining of the side skirt gores to the waist.

Cut the sleeves of this model three-quarter length or long and close-fitting, according to personal preference. For a three-quarter length sleeve, cut a cuff facing of satin that will be, when finished, about 4 inches wide. This may be shaped with the lower portion of the sleeve pattern.

Cut the collar out of a straight piece of satin that, when finished, will be about 4 inches wide and correspond in length with the neck measurement. Also, cut a facing of the dress material this same size and shape.

Construction.—Baste the under-arm seams of the waist; then turn under the lower edge of the side waist portions on the seam line and baste these to the side skirt sections. Next, turn the edges of the front skirt panel and the back full-length panel on the lines marked from the pattern, and baste these flat to the waist and side skirt sections. Leave the left skirt seam open at the top for a placket. Also, leave the left front waist line of the waist and the skirt panel free to provide an opening.

Fitting.—Observe, in addition to general fitting details, the width of the panels, and narrow the front panel toward the waist line and the back panel across the shoulders if to do so will make the figure appear to better advantage. If the dress shows any tendency to fall toward the front, try lifting it just a trifle at the back armhole, thus drawing it up at the sides and overcoming this difficulty.

As the collar of this dress does not roll over to cover the joining line in the back, the fitting of the dress at this point should be done with special care. If the panel does not fit up well around the neck, it will prove worth your while to remove the bastings that secure it to the remainder of the dress and lift the whole panel from ¼ to ¾ inch, depending on the alteration that is needed. Then mark the new neck line and pin the new shoulder line. See that the shoulder line does not drop at all beyond the shoulder point. The length of the shoulder regulates the height of the armhole curve, and unless this is brought well up on the shoulder much of the smartness and becomingness of the dress will be lost.

Finishing.—First mark the shoulder line very accurately and remove the bastings. Then stitch the under arms in a plain pressed-open seam and the waist and side-skirt portions in a narrow tucked seam. Next, stitch the panels on the wrong side, a seam's width from the raw edges, and finish the placket.

Apply the embroidery before proceeding any further. Be sure not to catch the stitches through the plaits and thus prevent their opening. Arrange the stitches so that they will appear in continuous rows when the plaits are laid flat. The illustration shows five long stitches on the upper portion of the plait and two stitches at the side, although there is a third stitch under the plait that is evident when the plait is open. If the sleeves are short, embroider them above the satin facing; if they are long, embroider the wrist edge.

Join the shoulder edges with a plain pressed-open seam. Then make the collar, turn back the portions allowed for front facings on the waist, and apply the collar as you would in attaching a similar collar to a plain blouse; that is, with all the seam edges to the inside of the collar.

At the center-front waist closing, work with buttonhole-stitches over small eyelet rings, so that a silk lacer may be run through, and finish the waist line of the left front to make a neat closing. Then make a tailored bow in the narrow girdle, tack this in position, and, in addition to securing snap fasteners along the dress closing, sew one under the bow in the girdle, so that this may be neatly fastened.

Model 7

Variations of Straight-Line Dress

Model 7A.—Recently several young women were trying to decide, if only one very nice dress could be bought, whether it should be of velvet, duvetyn, satin, or cloth. Finally, satin and cloth won on the point of appropriateness entirely, it being contended that velvet would not be appropriate on all occasions and that duvetyn would be too hard to keep brushed and pressed if worn to any great extent. But if one may have a cloth dress for general wear, then a velvet dress like Model 7A, which is indeed beautiful, would be fine for special occasions. This is made of black velvet, having bindings of silk braid and being trimmed with covered-cord rosettes formed of corded silk that, in texture, matches the braid. The vest is of pin-tucked Georgette, the portion that extends below the waist line being edged with self-ruffles.

A dainty net, silk-mull, or fine-tinted lace vest might be used in place of Georgette. The tinted laces make excellent trimming for dresses of velvet and satin. A black-velvet dress, for instance, with a turquoise-blue or a gold-lace vest of delicate texture would be very smart and pleasing.

For the dress, 4 yards of velvet will be sufficient, with ½ yard of Georgette or lace for the vest, 6½ yards of ⅝-inch braid for binding the front and back panels, the collar, and the sleeves, and ½ yard of corded silk for the covered-cord rosettes.

To make the rosettes, first cut bias strips of the corded silk and cover a cord of medium weight in the manner directed in your lessons. Then cut circular pieces of soft taffeta for a foundation, have the edges picoted, and, starting at the center of the foundation with a finished end of the cord, wind this in circular rows, placing these rows close together and securing them with rather long slip-stitches. Wind the last row of cord on the picoted edge in order to cover this, and secure the end of the cord under the foundation.

Model 7B.—This is a type of dress tempting to own because of its general becomingness and ever-readiness. Serge, tricotine, and Poiret twill seem to be the right fabrics, and navy seems to be the color, with ribbonzine embroidery in black, brown, or blue. The skirt is plain, yet delightfully dignified by its artistic embroidery, panels, and diagonal yoke lines. The narrow leather belt and surplice-shawl collar have their part, too, in making the dress thoroughly attractive.

The advisability of providing a leather belt should be considered before purchasing one, for such a belt, even though narrow, attracts attention to the waist line, and if, because of a large waist measurement, an inconspicuous finish is desired at this point, a narrow belt of self-material may be provided. The closing of such a belt may be given a tailored finish by a plain dark buckle or a foundation covered with self-material.

For the dress are required 3½ yards of 54-inch material, a small piece of Georgette, batiste, or organdie for the vestee, and eight button molds from ¾ to 1 inch in diameter.

Model 7C.—The ever-pleasing cartridge type of trimming is used on this dress of Poiret twill. This effect in trimming may be obtained in several ways—by means of ribbon having a definite crosswise cord, by material having tiny pin tucks arranged at close, regular intervals, by material that is plaited flat and bound with narrow ribbon or bias material to hold the plaits in position, or by the use of a recent novelty, namely, plaited woolen braid, which comes in all widths and many color schemes. The elongated shirtwaist-collar and basque front are also good features because of their youthful simplicity and almost invariable becomingness, and the box plaits, which are left open above the waist line and faced, provide an interesting method of adding to the skirt width and still maintaining to a degree the straight silhouette.

For the average figure, 3½ yards of 54-inch material will prove sufficient for this dress if the cutting is carefully planned.

Also, a 10-yard bolt of narrow ribbon for cartridge trimming and ⅜ yard of white or tan satin for the collar and cuffs will be required.

In cutting the material, provide for the long-waisted effect at the center front, and, for the side sections of the skirt, cut straight pieces of material about 20 inches wide. Face the upper edge of these sections before laying in the plaits. Finish the lower edge of the center front of the waist separate from the skirt, so that the closing may be arranged after the placket edges at the left side of the front panel have been fastened.

Model 7D.—Duvetyn cannot be considered as an especially practical fabric for making entire dresses, but because of its luxurious appearance and the softness of its texture it has real merit for trimming. One of the loveliest of the colors in which duvetyn is made is a soft henna. Probably this is why henna duvetyn was used for the vest and collar of this black-satin dress, although this fact alone could not have induced a decision, for, nowadays, when one considers the colors that combine well with black, henna is bound to head the list.

Silver-thread embroidery in an open, all-over design trims the outer vest portion, which is edged with triangular sections of satin. Again, the triangular trimming is evident at the lower edge of the overskirt and the sleeve.

For this dress, provide 4 yards of satin and ⅝ yard of duvetyn. Cut the upper portion of the side foundation gores required for the skirt out of China silk and join this along with the overskirt, which is cut about 6 inches wider, to the front and back panels. Make the sleeves practically straight, so that they will be wide at the lower edge; then take away several inches of this width by cutting out a section, as illustrated.

To make the pointed trimming, first have a strip of material about 2 inches wide hemstitched through the center. Then cut on the row of hemstitching to form strips 1 inch wide having one picoted edge. For each point, cut a piece 2 inches long. Then turn back two corners of this piece so that the ends are even with the unfinished edge and the picoted edges meet in the center of the piece. Before applying the facing to the edges where the trimming is desired, baste the triangular sections in position, so that the turned-back picoted edges do not show on the right side and the edges of the triangles just meet.

Arrange the closing of the dress at the left side front panel, and finish the right side of the vest so that it may come in position after the waist lining and the placket have been fastened.

Model 7E.—Of more than usual distinction is this model of navy serge and black satin, a combination of materials that has been tried and found lacking in no point of favor. But even the most practical, as well as desirable, fabrics are bound to become a trifle monotonous if they are brought to use in the same form season after season, and so, to create particular interest in this model, the joining of the band to the sleeve and of the waist to the side skirt portions is blended with a very attractive embroidery design developed in wool floss of greenish-blue and rust. Because of the number of seam lines in the waist and skirt and the limited amount of contrasting material necessary for developing the design, this style is an especially good one to follow in remodeling. In this case, the front and back panels may be pieced at the waist line, if necessary, and the piecing covered with a different arrangement of the belt.

For making this dress for the average figure, provide 1¾ yards of 54-inch serge, if you do not care to make the dress more than 50 or 52 inches wide at the lower edge, as well as 1⅛ yards of black satin and a bias strip of white satin or organdie about 8 inches wide and ⅝ yard long for the collar. Make the collar by folding this bias strip lengthwise through the center, holding the cut edges a trifle full when applying them, and then folding the collar over to form the effect illustrated.

7B

7A

7D

7C

7E

Overblouse Dress

Style.—This dress seems to need no emphasis as to its virtues, for like a beautiful stream or landscape it seems right for its place. The long waist, the Tuxedo collar and tunic-apron effect, with their appropriate embroidery, the cascade hip and combination sash—all give delightful expression of the mode. The plump woman may say, "beautiful for a slender figure, but not appropriate for me." But the cascade fulness over the hips can be easily omitted and the sash of the waist brought down on the figure and made less full. In this way an appearance of length may be provided, and the smart cascade and bouffant waist-line effect left for the new dress for the slender sister.

A survey of this Service will show a preference for dark colors and a majority of plain fabrics. And here, again, we must tell of a costume developed in dark color and of a plain fabric, but these features are so definitely the fashion and, as a rule, so much more becoming than lighter colors or figured materials that we are glad to encourage them.

The popularity of plain fabrics may be credited entirely to the dominance of velvet and luxurious satin. These two materials are perhaps the most beautiful of all materials and this season rightly occupy the choice place in the wardrobe. A deep-brown velvet with gold embroidery and a pale corn-color vest, a brown-velvet turban with corn-color aigrette, brown suède shoes, and deep-ivory kid gloves would indeed make a sumptuous costume. Or, brown or blue satin, black, henna, or taupe velvet—any of these colors in soft, rich material would make possible a beautiful dress for afternoon wear if developed according to this model.

The embroidery, in almost every instance, should be delicate in design, preferably of dull gold or silver. For the embroidery pattern, try imitating the original design on light-weight paper. Practice until you get a good outline; then you can trace this as many times as you desire and baste the tracing over the material to be embroidered. Place the embroidery stitches right over the pattern, for the tissue paper can be pulled away when the design is complete. One precaution that should be observed in the making of any dress is to let much of its beauty be dependent on its simplicity; watch carefully that you do not overtrim.

Kimono or set-in sleeves may be used; the latter, however, will prove safer in the heavy, soft materials, with the exception of velvets. The set-in sleeve is pleasing in this type of dress, as it gives a good balance line with the cascade lines in the skirt. If the kimono sleeve is used, then perhaps a panel back will prove desirable. If set-in sleeves are provided, the panel will not be so necessary.

Material and Pattern.—For an average figure, 5 yards of 40-inch material is required to develop this dress. A piece of Georgette, fine lace, or net 12 inches square is sufficient for the vest. The waist portion of McCall pattern No. 9395 may be used as a guide in cutting the waist of this design, although several changes will be required in the development of the muslin to make it an exact duplicate. In cutting the muslin waist model, leave surplus material below the waist line of the pattern so that this may be draped on the figure to give just the desired effect.

For the skirt, cut two skirt lengths of material. Then make provision for the cascade effect by forming a half-bias seam edge on both sides of each of these sections, tapering them from the full 40-inch width at the top to a 26-inch width at the lower edge. This will make the skirt a trifle less than 2¼ yards at the top and 1½ yards at the lower edge.

If the width of the material you are using is not sufficient to permit ample fulness at the waist line and in the cascade portions by cutting the material in this manner, cut sections for the cascades separate from the skirt. These may be inserted in the side seams and will not prove at all objectionable. Form the pattern for the separate cascade by experimenting with muslin.

For the apron, cut a straight piece 24 inches wide and four-fifths of the skirt length; this will make the width about two-thirds of the length. In cutting the collar, sash, and apron edges, allow at least ¾ inch to be turned back in the finish. Provide for the cuff a bias strip of material about 5½ inches wide and 3 inches longer than the width at the lower edge of the sleeve.

Construction.—Join the half-bias seam edges of the skirt section by means of a plain seam. Also, stitch the waist-line edges together from the side seams for a distance of about 10 inches, to provide a finish for that portion of the waist line which is to be left free to form the upper edge of the cascade effect. Then either press or steam these seams open, according to the kind of material you are working with. Clip away the surplus material at the corner so that when this section is turned right side out a very flat finish will result and the corner will not be bulky. Arrange for the opening of the skirt at the left side front so that it will be concealed with the apron, and finish this with a continuous placket.

Skirt lengths varying from 7 to 12 inches from the floor are now in evidence. This ample latitude is given so that one may choose the length that is most becoming from the viewpoint of age, type, and even the style of the dress, for a model with a long tunic requires a slightly longer foundation than would prove becoming in another design.

If you are making the dress of velvet, finish the waist, collar, cuff, sash, and apron edges by turning them back ¾ inch, or the allowance made in cutting, and without turning under the raw edge of the velvet, catch-stitching them with comparatively loose stitches. Use sufficient care in doing this work to prevent the edge from appearing drawn and the stitches from showing on the right side.

In finishing satin or soft taffeta, first have the extreme edges hemstitched and cut close to the hemstitching; then turn the edges back and catch-stitch them down with the same precautions regarding the stitches. Gather the upper edge of the vest and bind it with a narrow strip of self-material.

If you wish to make a particularly nice finish for the collar, cuffs, girdle ends, and apron section, line them with Georgette crêpe of a matching color, slip-stitching the lining close to the inner edge of the turned-back portion.

Adjust the fulness of the skirt to the stay belt of the waist lining, which has been cut to come just outside of the vest line of the waist so that it will not show under the sheer material. Adjust the cascade effect in the skirt, and to hold this in position properly tack it at several intervals to a tape suspended from the waist line underneath, tacking so that the stitches will be concealed under the folds of the cascade. Then secure the apron effect in position.

Next pin the vest to the lining; then put the blouse on over the lining and adjust the vest to occupy the right space. Drape the girdle and plan where the blouse portion should be tacked to the lining; usually this is done at the shoulder and the waist line. Some prefer to have the blouse entirely separate, contending that it has an easier appearance when entirely free from the lining. But even if the blouse is not secured to the lining, do not omit it, for it provides a smooth foundation and serves as a protection to the dress.

To form the cuff effect that is illustrated, bring the bands, which have been previously finished, around the lower edge of the sleeve and lap them in reverse of their usual position; then pin and tack them in place on the plain sleeve, which has first been finished by means of a turned-back catch-stitched edge.

Model 9

Variations of Overblouse Dress

Model 9A.—For business and practical wear, the two-piece dress runs in close competition with the one-piece dress. There is perhaps a little more grace in the two-piece dress because the skirt length remains stationary, while the dress or overblouse portion sways itself with the movements of the body. Then, too, this dress gives a more comfortable and pleasing skirt length when sitting down, because the skirt drops more quickly and permanently into position. Strive for simplicity always in making dresses for much wear, for they will prove more becoming and stay smart and good to look at very much longer than if made elaborate in design or decoration. If you can have but few dresses, make simplicity in dress your hobby. Your friends will congratulate you and in your own heart you will know that you are better dressed than ever before.

To meet the requirements of those who desire a very simple type of dress, this model was chosen. The odd cuff effect supplies one detail that removes the style from the ordinary class, but the principal interest is the vest of contrasting color so attractively embroidered.

The material used for this particular model is couture-brown faille, having a rather heavy rib. The vest is of a harmonious shade of tan duvetyn, embroidered in various shades of brown with just a touch of medium-bright blue. For the average stout woman, this would be a good model, but for extremely large figures so much emphasis should not be placed on the vest. Instead, use self-material embroidered in self-color.

It is not difficult to find a pattern that may be used with little or no change to duplicate this model. For instance, McCall design No. 9140 has very much the same lines, but the waist is made in kimono effect instead of with a set-in sleeve. Pictorial Review pattern No. 8255 features the set-in sleeve, which, of course, is preferable for a stout figure.

For the average figure, 5 yards of 36- or 40-inch material with ¼ yard of trimming for the vest section will prove sufficient. Before cutting the dress, determine just what length in the tunic portion will prove most becoming to you. Also, decide whether the collar, which is extended to form a trimming band the entire length of the overdress, may be broadened or narrowed just a trifle in order to make it more suitable for you. Follow closely the instructions given on the pattern envelope for placing the different pattern pieces on the material, for an overblouse as long as this will not be at all satisfactory unless cut on the correct grain. You may make the underskirt entirely of self-material, or cut the upper part of the back gore from China silk or light-weight lining material. Arrange the placket of the skirt at the left side seam, and secure the skirt as well as the waist lining to an inside stay belt. Make the overblouse entirely separate, and arrange the closing at the left side of the vest.

Finish the lower edge of the sleeve with a narrow binding of self-material. Then, to form the cuff effect that is illustrated, cut two lengthwise strips of material, making them about 15 inches long and 2½ inches wide. Seam each of these strips and face them with very soft silk or Georgette crêpe that matches exactly the color of the dress. With the strips finished in this manner, tack them to the lower edge of the sleeve.

Model 9B.—Crêpe de Chine in a medium shade of neutral gray relies in this model solely on gray-silk tassels and blue wool embroidery for trimming. The embroidery on the skirt consists merely of three rows of darning-stitches, and the same stitch is carried out on the trimming bands in the waist portion, although a more interesting design is developed in this case. Because of the shorter overblouse portion, the style is not so well suited to the stout as the medium type of figure. If the overblouse is lengthened in making a dress for a stout person, the tassels should be omitted, in order to make the design, as a whole, pleasing and well-balanced.

The same pattern that is used for Model 9A may be employed in cutting this design, but the quantity of material required may be diminished from ¼ to ½ yard. Finish the slashed opening at the center front of the vest by facing it with a narrow strip of self-material.

Model 9C.—Is there anything quite so comfort-giving in one's wardrobe as a navy-blue silk frock that is rather simple in design? It is ever ready to solve the problem of what to wear when one is in doubt as to the appropriateness of a dressy gown and yet hesitates to appear in the ordinary type of street or afternoon dress. No matter what the nature of the occasion may be, the blue dress is not conspicuous as either a formal or an informal extreme; consequently, it commands a great deal of one's respect and appreciation that almost verges on devotion.

This navy-blue model with its harem skirt partly revealed under six straight "flying" panels and its surplice, drop-shoulder overblouse is of crêpe meteor and seems perfectly content with no other trimming than its bindings of self-colored grosgrain ribbon. The back panel effect has a great deal of character because of the manner in which it is inserted in the overblouse.

The waist pattern that is used for cutting the feature dress will serve very well for the development of this style, but, of course, it will be necessary to mark the back panel effect on the pattern and make extra provision for this in cutting the material. Finish the slashed opening for the lower edge of the back waist panel by facing it with self-material in much the same manner as you would apply a facing in the development of a bound buttonhole. Cut the harem skirt straight, and finish it at the lower edge in the manner previously directed. Make the loose, or "flying," panels of straight strips of material 7 or 8 inches wide and 4 or 5 inches less than you desire the finished skirt length.

Model 9D.—This season Fashion has offered such a bewildering array of exquisite fabrics that one is not surprised to find the drapery that forms the overskirt of this model made entirely of gold-and-black brocade. The brocade is very effectively set off by an underskirt and a bodice of gold cloth, and also by the arrangement of flame-colored tulle, which is looped up at the back-waist line to form a sort of sash effect and extended to give the semblance of a train. This dress may be very successfully developed in other materials, however. For instance, soft chiffon taffeta in a bright, becoming color might be combined with lace for the underskirt and bodice, or a figured silk combined with plain might be used to excellent advantage.

For a drapery of this style, 2½ yards of 36- or 40-inch material will prove sufficient. It will be necessary, also, to provide 2½ yards of fabric to be used for the underskirt and bodice and 1½ yards of tulle if you desire to make the train of this material. Pictorial Review waist pattern No. 8182 has lines similar to the blouse of this design, but it is cut somewhat lower and worn with a straight underbodice. It would be a simple matter, however, to build up the surplice lines of the pattern to make them suitable for this style.

To form the pattern for the skirt drapery, experiment with muslin. Let the lengthwise grain run around the figure, and begin the drapery by pinning one crosswise end at the center back so that about 28 or 30 inches of it extends below the waist line. Draw the material down at the left side in order to make it assume the deep folds that are illustrated and pin it up at the right side so that it will extend only a little more than half the skirt length. Then, drop the material toward the center back, and cut it on a decidedly diagonal line to form the pointed effect that is illustrated. The drapery may be arranged so that the selvage edge of the material will form the lower edge. It will therefore be unnecessary to shape this, other than to round off the corner that meets the pointed end at the center back.

9A

9B

9C

9D

Deep-Collar Coat

In a dress-up coat, coziness is as essential as becomingness, and it seems that these two features usually go together; but the friendly warmth of a winter coat should ever be a first consideration. Whether a coat is bought outright, custom made, or made at home, it should possess: first, warmth; second, becomingness; and third, as much luxuriousness as purse or time, or both, will permit.

A prominent designer is quoted as saying that "a coat will sell if it has a big, generous cozy collar, even though it is not in the least prepared for warmth or wear." The deep collars are very much appreciated. They are smart and becoming and seem to lend just the right rightness to a coat, especially when handsome material and decoration are available.

Coats, like tunics, are from 2 to 4 inches above the skirt's lower edge. If your dress has a tunic, plan to have your coat long enough to come over the tunic edge, so that there will be no confused lines. Smartness from "tip to toe" is good advice. Consider every detail, so that your entire costume will help you to exemplify perfection.

During the past few seasons, the use of soft, luxurious materials has been growing more pronounced until, at the present time, this vogue is at its height. Duvetyn and even more beautiful fabrics of similar or novelty weave are found in a great many models, but for service broadcloth, unless it is of a very fine quality, velour, Silvertone, and tricotine are more commendable and really may be employed with excellent results.

Colors in woolen coat fabrics include navy, green, grayed blues of medium and dark tones, brown in rather deep shades, as well as the golden variety, brick, slightly grayed green, and a group of colors that range from gray to tan.

Coats and suits this season carry beautiful linings that are soft in texture and often very striking in design and colorings. Sometimes the linings appear almost gaudy, they are so bright and unusual. Such linings are appropriate for some coats, but not for your one coat that must be worn with different colored dresses. It is always confusing to remove a coat that has a lining out of harmony with the dress or blouse. The linings extend throughout in dress-up coats; in sport coats, through the sleeves, shoulders, and bust only.

The models made for first-grade shops have a light-wool interlining in the upper sleeve portion, extending to 2 inches above the elbow, and through the bust and shoulders, terminating about 3 inches above the waist line. Interlinings of canvas are omitted entirely, even in the coat fronts, but in some instances, very soft, open-weave muslin is used in its place to serve as a stay.

When embroidery is used for such coats, it is usually inclined to indefinite lines and is almost invariably done in self-color; that is, a color exactly the same as the coat itself. Wool embroidery is frequently used for coats, but not so much as the heavy silk floss and ribbonzine embroidery. When the softer, more expensive qualities of cloth are used for a coat, the buttons are generally covered with self-fabric, but other materials, such as velour and Silvertone, are trimmed with novelty buttons of various shapes and kinds.

The model illustrated, which is of beaver-colored duvetyn, is embroidered in self-color silk floss with glove-stitching across the front to relieve the plainness and to carry the embroidery effect from collar to hips. This is a point in design. Can you visualize the abruptness if this connection were not made?

Material and Pattern.—The average figure requires about 3¾ yards of 54-inch material for this style. If a lining is desired, 4 yards of 40-inch material, such as a very soft satin or crêpe de Chine, should also be provided.

Home pattern No. 2712, which may be had in sizes for women and misses, may be used for cutting a design similar to this style. Of course, it will be advisable for you to check up this pattern with your individual measurements and cut and fit a muslin model very carefully, so that little or no change will be required in fitting the coat itself. In placing the pattern sections on the material, be guided by the diagram on the back of the pattern envelope. Also, do not fail to follow the perforations, which should be placed on a lengthwise thread, for the grain of each section of any tailored garment must run correctly if satisfactory results are obtained.

When cutting the right front of the coat, fold back the front edge of the pattern to provide for a trimming band about 3½ inches wide. Cut the cuffs of a straight piece of material, so that when finished they will be about 5 inches wide and extend 3 inches beyond the sleeve. Develop a collar pattern of muslin by placing a lengthwise edge at the neck line, gathering in the fulness across the back and laying two or three small plaits diagonally from each side front. These plaits will merge into the collar fulness and not be evident when the collar is buttoned up around the neck. When you have made the muslin fit correctly at the neck line, cut the outline of the collar to make it the shape you desire.

If you wish to make a lining, cut it with the aid of the coat pattern and provide a 1-inch plait at the center back.

Construction.—Turn under the seam allowance made on the right front edge of the upper portion of the coat, baste the trimming band in position, and then join the seams as directed in the pattern instructions, making the seams plain and then pressing them open and slashing them to prevent them from drawing. Too much care cannot be exercised in the making of a garment such as this, for unless each detail is made exact and given the proper attention, the general appearance of the coat will be marred.

Duvetyn requires very special care in handling, and it should be used only by those who have had a great deal of experience in working with woolen materials as well as velvets, for it has qualities similar to each. Precautions that must be observed in working with duvetyn are: Steam rather than press the seams and any other parts that may require such attention; then shake out the material while it is still a trifle damp in order to bring the warp up. Avoid handling the fabric and thus forming finger prints when it is damp; also, handle the seams as little as possible during the process of making. Employ hand sewing with silk thread whenever practical, and in stitching on the machine use a comparatively loose tension, for the thickness of the fabric takes up the stitches and tends to make the seam appear tight when stitched under ordinary tension.

Finishing.—Make the covered-cord loops to be used for the fastening, and before stitching the front facing, insert the ends of the loops in the seam that joins the facing to the coat. Also, work the rows of glove-stitch embroidery on the center-front trimming band before securing the facing back in position, and then apply the embroidery to the remainder of the coat.

Join the collar to the coat by turning under the neck edge of the coat and basting this flat to the gathered edge of the collar. Bring the neck edge of the front facing up over the seam to conceal it at the front, and cover the remainder of the seam with a facing cut in cape effect about 2 inches wide and shaped with the neck portion of the coat pattern or with the lining, provided one is desired in the coat.

Finish the lower edge of the sleeve with a narrow silk binding; then tack the cuff, which has been made according to previous instructions, to the sleeve, arranging it at just the point desired.

*Look for a collectible print version
at the end of this issue.*

Model 10

Coats and Suits

Model 10A.—In thinking over the coats and dresses you have had during the past few years, you will probably recall quite vividly several models that were particularly satisfactory and serviceable, garments that you did not tire of quickly, and that, because of their conservativeness, seemed to lose little of their style value from season to season. Recollection of these "stand-bys" will probably cause you to make your decision for a coat style in favor of this particular model, which is of a heavy blue-and-gray mixture, a fabric that will not readily show either dust or soil. This season's trimming offering is evidenced in the rows of gray chenille stitching and the soft-gray leather belt. This model would be very smart also if made of dark-blue tricotine and trimmed with deep-plum or turquoise-blue wool embroidery, either of these combinations proving effective where so scant an amount of color is used.

For this style, 4¼ yards of 44-inch material will be sufficient for the average figure. The same Home pattern that was mentioned as being suitable for the deep-collar coat might be used for this style, with the lower portion of the coat made of separate strips or practically the same effect produced by rows of stitching arranged horizontally.

Model 10B.—Although loose-back coat models have had a season of popularity, they are by no means out of fashion, for their youthfulness and becomingness to many types will undoubtedly keep them in favor for some time. Swamp green, a medium, grayed color, was chosen in velour for this model, and the suggestion of embroidery, which indicates the waist line of the loose back, is carried out in a slightly darker shade of green-wool floss. An elaborate embroidery design used in such a manner would not harmonize well with the general style, but the simple band effect seems to add just the right touch.

Other than the loose back, the extension of the center-front trimming band, and the turn-back cuffs, this model has practically the same lines as the deep-collar coat and, therefore, may be cut with the aid of the same pattern.

To arrange the back portion of the pattern in order to make it suitable for this model, first mark the broad panel effect and also a shallow, round yoke, provided you desire to have the back quite full through the shoulder portion. Cut the pattern on the panel line, also on the yoke line if one has been drawn; then slash the back section lengthwise at several points and separate the pieces when placing them on the material in order to provide the amount of flare you desire. In cutting, extend the panel full coat length.

Suit Tendencies.—Long, straight lines prevail, whenever possible, in today's fashions. Perhaps they are offered to help the many, many women who possess more pounds than fashion artists like to depict. And such women recognize, as do the artists, that the straight lines help not only the individual but her friends to forget that she carries more pounds than are actually becoming.

In the majority of coat suits, the waist line is only slightly fitted, although some declare that ere the winter is definitely here, suit coats will be actually "nipped-in" at the waist line. This scarcely seems probable when it is considered that every new model presented comes a wee bit nearer the skirt hem, and one of the prime requisites of a "nipped-in" coat is that it stop short from 2 to 12 inches below the waist line. Some interesting suits have the coats terminating midway of the skirt length; other styles choose a three-quarter length; and still others do not seem content without rivaling the top coat, for they reach almost to the lower edge of the skirt.

In some models, the waist line is marked with a narrow band of cartridge plaits; others have a very narrow belt of self-material or leather; while others boast of no belt, hanging in box effect straight down from the shoulders.

One may choose from a variety of fabrics in making a suit selection, for the list includes tricotine, cheviot, broadcloth, velour, duvetyn, velveteen, and velvet, as well as novelty suitings and soft rich weaves of various descriptions.

Black is very popular in velvet, velveteen, and many of the softer woolens. As for colors, a somewhat wider range is evidenced in suits than is shown in coat models.

Model 10C.—Simplicity, the prime essential of a service suit, is happily introduced in this fur-collared model, the original of which was developed in bluish, elephant-gray broadcloth and trimmed in ⅜-inch dark blue Hercules braid. The lining is of soft-gray silk three shades lighter than the suit material.

To develop this suit for the average figure, 3¼ yards of 54-inch material is used, with 2⅓ yards of 36-inch lining and 8 yards of braid. McCall coat pattern No. 8623 has lines that are quite similar to this design and may be used satisfactorily in cutting it. In order to make the coat assume comparatively straight lines, take out the ripple that is evident in the McCall pattern by laying in a few shallow plaits at its lower edge.

Cut the skirt with the aid of a plain, straight pattern that has the panel effect marked on the front. Provide for no other seams in the skirt than those which join the panel. One length of 54-inch fabric will prove sufficient for cutting the skirt in this manner, for the width at the lower edge may be less than 1½ yards.

Join the skirt sections with plain seams, and lay a 1½-inch plait along the panel edge. Provide a placket under the plait at the left side.

Finish the coat edges by turning them back and catch-stitching them, being sure not to take the stitches through to the outer side of the fabric. The catch-stitching will be covered with the lining when this is properly secured in position.

Model 10D.—Tailored suits, from the most severe to the elaborate models, have such a decided service value that fashion never fails to give considerable attention to them, although some seasons more emphasis is laid on separate coats than on suits, because of the general trend of styles. This season one would naturally suppose that separate coats, which have been made more luxurious and less ordinary than ever before, would relegate suits to the background. But such assumptions are without foundation, for suits are maintaining a goodly share of popular favor, and in regard to fabric and design they have no difficulty in holding equal footing with separate coats. Perhaps the very lovely overblouses that are shown have much to do with the favor accorded suits, especially the dressier models, for the combination of the two prepares one for many afternoon and evening functions.

Embroidery, of course, is evident on most of the elaborate suits, as shown in this model of rust-colored duvetyn embroidered with heavy self-colored silk floss and silver threads. The self-collar is made doubly attractive by means of the kerchief treatment, and the cuffs, which are a modification of a style shown previously in this Service, are all that one could desire as an appropriate sleeve finish.

For this suit, 5¼ yards of 36-inch material is required, with 1½ yards of China silk for the skirt foundation. The same pattern that is suggested for Model 10C may be used as a foundation for cutting the coat of this design. Note the arrangement of the trimming bands and also the front closing, which overlaps its entire length rather than meets merely at the neck line as in the McCall pattern. Form the kerchief effect with a bias strip of material, first experimenting with muslin to produce the desired result.

Cut the tunic with the aid of a plain, straight-skirt pattern, arranging seams at the sides and making the width at the lower edge about 1¾ yards.

10 C

10 B

10 D

10 a

Wraps or Capes

Generosity seems to be the word that describes better than any other the wraps that have been introduced for fall and winter. This quality is evident not only in the kind of fabric and its use, but also in the collars, which are extremely high and unstintedly full in almost all wraps except those of the sport type, and, again, in the lavish use of hand embroidery, which seems to have no limit once it is started.

Wraps seem to have the faculty of carrying the extremes. They may be made of ermine luxuriously lined; they may weigh pounds and pounds; and, again, they may be of fairy lightness, made of finest nets, tulles, malines, and chiffons. It is beautiful to see the exquisite color effects often produced by means of these transparent wraps. Chief among the fabrics that are more appropriate for a little more ordinary wear are duvetyn and dovedown, for these materials have the soft, clinging texture so desirable at present. Even more serviceable, however, are the wraps of velour, Silvertone, and broadcloth.

Linings are all that one could desire in regard to variety, beauty, and richness of color and quality of texture. Naturally, lining materials are of the very softest quality because of the wrap materials with which they are used. The Pussy-willow silks, satin, crêpe meteor, crêpe de Chine, and even Georgette crêpe are numbered among the favored fabrics. Figured linings, which are more in evidence than plain ones, are quite unusual in character, and afford an opportunity to indulge in pretentious designs and bright colors that for other purposes might not be strictly in accordance with one's conservative ideas.

Interlinings in wraps depend on the warmth and the effect desired. Duvetyn appears easier and more graceful without an interlining. Satin seems more luxurious when an interlining is used; in fact, it seems necessary for this material.

The oval, or egg-shaped, silhouette is dominant in wraps. The reasons for this are perhaps the pleasing innovation afforded in variance from the straight-line effect and also the narrow width in which many of the more elegant fabrics are made. For instance, duvetyn, like chiffon velvet, is made in 36- and 40-inch widths.

Wraps, as a general rule, do not permit any other glimpse of the dress worn underneath than that portion which extends below the lower edge. The skirt portion comes from 2 to 4 inches above the bottom of the dress skirts.

Model 11A.—To be extremely practical, a wrap that is intended for a general-utility garment, that is, for wear on the street with afternoon frocks or possibly as a substitute for an evening cloak, should be of a color that is unobtrusive and that combines satisfactorily with almost any other color. Also, the material should be of a kind that will stand service well and not require a great deal of care to keep it in a presentable condition. This design is expressive of these very features, for it is made of a soft, durable quality of wool velour in admiral, which is a deep shade of blue. The trimming of embroidery in a rather dark-gray wool further emphasizes the conservativeness of the model, while the lining of soft satin, also of gray but lighter than that of the embroidery, would set off, or at least appear harmonious with, any costume when the wrap is thrown back from the shoulders.

This style of wrap requires, for the average figure, 3¼ yards of 54-inch material. It may be cut with the aid of McCall pattern No. 9734 as a foundation, for the lines of this pattern are practically the same as this model.

In the construction of the cape, join the sections with plain seams, press these seams open, and clip them at close intervals through the curved portions so that they will be flat.

Before slashing the material to make openings for the hands, place over the line marked for the slash a straight strip of self-colored silk that is about 2½ inches wide and 1½ inches longer than the marked line. Stitch this a scant ¼ inch each side of the line; then slash through the strip and the wrap, turn the facing piece on the stitched seam line to the wrong side, and baste this securely in position. Leave the edges of the strip free if you intend to place a lining in the wrap, but if the wrap is to be without a lining, turn under the edges and secure them with fine, loose hemming-stitches. Pay particular attention to the finish at each end of the strip in order to make it as flat as possible and very neat. Next, finish the trimming band that is intended to cover the slashed opening. Face this with self-material or with soft silk of a matching color, provided the wrap material is extremely heavy. Then either stitch or slip-stitch the finished trimming band to the outside or upper edge of the opening, so that it will extend toward the center front and cover the opening, as the illustration shows.

A collar of the type shown in this model needs to be lined throughout in order that it will hold up well around the neck. Therefore, make the collar of two thicknesses of self-material or line it with silk. If you use silk, choose Pussy willow, crêpe meteor, or something similar, so that its extreme softness will prevent it from interfering with the style effect of the collar.

In finishing the wrap, tack the girdle at both openings, letting this extend underneath the back of the cape and permitting the ends to be adjusted at the center front.

Model 11B.—When one has a coat that will serve very well for ordinary occasions, it is not necessary that utility be given foremost consideration in the selection of a wrap. Instead, one may indulge in a fabric and a lining that satisfy in every respect one's preference in regard to color and texture. The style also may be a trifle more extreme than should be chosen for a general-utility wrap.

This model is an example of the popular semidressy wrap. It is of wood-colored duvetyn, with large embroidery motifs developed with silk floss that matches exactly the color of the duvetyn. The brown note is carried further in the trimming of fur on the collar, and again in the lining, which has a deep cream-colored background with figures in any number of brown shades enhanced by sprinklings of turquoise blue.

A wrap such as this with a deep collar and cape requires, for the average figure, 5¼ yards of 36- or 40-inch duvetyn, ¾ yard of silk of matching color, and 3 yards of lining material. It may be cut with the aid of the pattern used for Model 11A, as this pattern includes also an overcape.

In cutting a wrap from material as narrow as 36 or 40 inches, it is generally advisable to remove a little width from the lower edge of the pattern by laying it in darts, rather than to provide piecings for the side seams, which would prove conspicuous and mar the appearance of the finished garment.

Make the overcape of only one thickness of material, and face the lower edge with a ⅜- to 2-inch bias facing in silk that matches the cape perfectly. Line the collar throughout with silk like that used for the cape facing.

Model 11C.—Quite out of the ordinary is this design with its double collar and cape, the main part of the model being of neutral-gray dovedown and the under collar and cape of an excellent quality of satin in a deeper shade of gray. The embroidery and tassels that finish the points formed at the side back further emphasize the neutral color scheme. But the real surprise comes when the wrap is thrown back and exposes a lining that is as variegated in color as an old-fashioned garden.

This style, which may be cut with the aid of the pattern previously discussed, requires 5¼ yards of dovedown, 1½ yards of satin, and 3 yards of lining material. In finishing, the edges of both the satin and the dovedown may be picoted.

11a

11B

11C

*W*HEN the curtain of style expectancy parted to reveal Fashion's newest triumph in dress creation, among the first models to appear was one that might have been inspired by anticipated beauties of very early fall. As shown at the lower right, the coloring of its waist portion, orange crêpe Roma with all-over gold embroidery in delicate vein work, and a touch of leaf green carried out in the sash and sleeve banding, give a marked suggestion of frost-brightened foliage. The black velvet skirt and mink banding are in tribute to winter fashion predictions.

Just above is a fall dance frock of black satin, its close basque softened with an exquisite lace bertha and its very full skirt overlaid at the center front with coral-colored ribbon panels suspended from lovely flowers of the same color.

Sufficiently versatile in character to complete an afternoon costume or to enfold the luxuriousness of an evening gown, the lovely wrap, as illustrated, is of toast and Mandalay duvetyn, embroidered over the lower side portions in honeycomb effect and collared in brown wolf.

Toast color is also the selection of the Canton crêpe dress with plaited panels, the panels on the skirt extending from triangular trimming motifs formed by interlaced strips of self-material.

Standing on Fashion's threshold, as if eagerly awaiting very formal midwinter functions, the striking model of black chiffon velvet with surplice banding of spotless ermine is truly a regal interpretation of the 1922 draped mode.

Magic Pattern: *Glamour Cape & Hood*

This is an original Magic Pattern, a project you cut out using diagrams instead of pattern pieces. These were first created by Mary Brooks Picken for the Woman's Institute's student magazines, Inspiration and Fashion Service. My book **Vintage Notions: An Inspirational Guide to Needlework, Cooking, Sewing, Fashion & Fun** featured 12 original Magic Patterns. Recently I have created modern patterns that were inspired by these vintage gems featured in the book **The Magic Pattern Book**, which I licensed with Workman Publishing. We have chosen to keep the authenticity of this original pattern intact and therefore have not changed instructions based on modern fabrics and techniques. Note at the end of this pattern you will find helpful tips for drafting pattern pieces.

The cape and hood of filmy lace and net can be worn everywhere – at cocktail parties, in restaurants, even at the theatre. They are flattering, less expensive than hats, and easier to manage when dining or dancing.

This lace cape with hood was made from ¾ yd. of 35" gossamer-type lace and 2 yds. of ½" wide velvet ribbon.

Take a piece of paper 27" x 36" and make a pattern. Fold in half lengthwise and lay fold toward you. Place point A at left-hand lower corner, as in diagram. Mark B 3" above A. Locate E halfway between upper corners C and D. F is halfway between E and D; G is same distance below D that F is to left of D. Draw a curved line B to E, F to G. Cut on these lines.

Put the hood on; bring it over hair as you want it. Tie ribbon around the neck over the lace, pin lace to ribbon. Line will come about as dotted line shows.

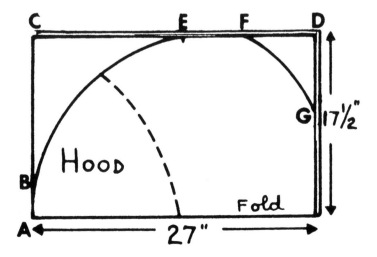

Finish edge of cape and hood by stitching edge 1/8" from edge all around; do this over paper to prevent tightening of stitching line. Turn stitched edge, making a rolled hem, and whip this down, or take to your local sewing shop and have all the edges picoted. Gather fullness under ribbon. Do not make this tight, as it should appear loose and easy. Tack ends of ribbon at edge of hood so that they will hold.

Your Measurement Chart & Notes on Making Magic Patterns

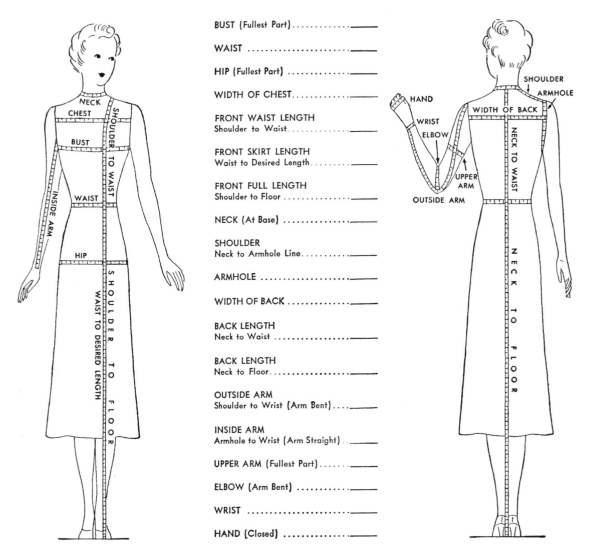

BUST (Fullest Part)............_____

WAIST ...._____

HIP (Fullest Part) ...._____

WIDTH OF CHEST............_____

FRONT WAIST LENGTH
Shoulder to Waist............_____

FRONT SKIRT LENGTH
Waist to Desired Length........._____

FRONT FULL LENGTH
Shoulder to Floor ...._____

NECK (At Base) ...._____

SHOULDER
Neck to Armhole Line.........._____

ARMHOLE ...._____

WIDTH OF BACK ...._____

BACK LENGTH
Neck to Waist ...._____

BACK LENGTH
Neck to Floor.................._____

OUTSIDE ARM
Shoulder to Wrist (Arm Bent)...._____

INSIDE ARM
Armhole to Wrist (Arm Straight).._____

UPPER ARM (Fullest Part)......._____

ELBOW (Arm Bent) ...._____

WRIST ...._____

HAND (Closed) ...._____

Keep Accurate Measurements

Since the garments in this book are all cut from measurements, it is necessary to have accurate ones to follow. Keep a list of your own measurements always at hand for ready reference.

Measurements for fitted garments should be taken over the type of foundation garments you expect to wear with them. Remove dress, jacket, or coat, which would distort the measurements. Do not take measurements too tight. Make all easy enough for comfort. The chart shows how to place the tape correctly for each measurement.

Making The Pattern

If you have the least doubt about your ability to chalk out garment on your fabric, then rough it out first with crayon heavy pencil on wrapping paper or newspaper. Cut out the pa pattern and use it to cut your garment. Cutting from a diagr you can be sure that the proportions are correct for your size that the garment will be a good fit.

If you enjoyed this issue of *Inspirations—Vintage Notions Monthly*, visit AmyBarickman.com for my curated collection of vintage content including patterns and books for needle and thread, inspiring fabrics and textiles and free vintage art every Friday. Be sure to tune in to *Vintage Notions* video episodes for a guided tour through my collection of sewing and fashion history, as well as modern projects inspired by my extensive library.

www.amybarickman.com

ind free images, inspiration and books for the sewing and needle arts!

www.indygojunction.com

Featuring digital & print patterns, books, tutorials, giveaways, project ideas, & more!

Subscribe to each of our eNewsletters to learn about new products, receive special offers, discounts, videos, and get a FREE eBook!

Inspiration Vintage Notions Monthly , Volume 1, Issue 1 (VN0101)

For wholesale ordering information contact Amy Barickman, LLC at 913.341.5559 or amyb@amybarickman.com, P.O. Box 30238, Kansas City, MO 64112

Made in the USA
Middletown, DE
07 March 2016